THE STRUGGLE OF SOCIAL ANXIETY

Stop The Awkwardness and Fear of Talking to People or Being Social. Proven Methods to Stop Social Anxiety and Achieve Self-Confidence, Even if You're Very Shy

Table of Contents

Introduction

Congratulations on Purchasing *Social Anxiety: Guide to Overcome Anxiety and Shyness*—and thank you for doing so!

Depression and anxiety are common mental health concerns that affect millions of people of all ages, genders, and races. Each diagnosis is unique to the person, and there are many treatment options and combinations of treatments that can make a difference. Depression can be treated, and someone who is depressed can find a way out of it.

There are many misconceptions when it comes to understanding the nuances of depression, phobias, and anxiety disorders. These misconceptions often paint the illness in a negative light. The truth is that everyone has fears. Everyone feels stressed. Everyone has moments in which the demands of life weigh heavily on their shoulders. Depression has many causes, and no person with this diagnosis will have the same symptoms or reactions.

This guide is meant to be a helpful and informative book that explains these complicated diagnoses in simple terms. While a guide like this should not replace the advice of a trained medical or mental health professional, helping people understand what depression is and how it can be managed provides hope to those who struggle daily to overcome this condition.

The following chapters will provide an insight into depression and social anxiety—two of the most common mental health diagnoses— and will provide suggestions and tips on how to manage depression and social anxiety. Other chapters will discuss techniques that supplement a formal treatment plan and focus on achieving a healthy mind and body as well as how to best utilize family and friends to work towards the lifting of depression.

There is a portion of the book that talks about the seriousness of depression. It covers the consequences to health because of the depressed mind, and it talks about suicide and the myths that obstruct better understanding of this very real consequence of depression. Addictions and self-harm also manifest when depression is undiagnosed and untreated.

There are plenty of books on this subject on the market—thanks again for choosing this one! Every effort was made to ensure it is full of as much useful information as possible. Please enjoy!

Chapter 1: Understanding Anxiety and Social Anxiety

The mind is a marvelous part of the human experience. It controls life functions, and it stores memories—it allows us to learn, to speak, to see, to experience life. It processes emotions, allows us to reason, and carries recollections of our triumphs and our tragedies. Its capabilities are limitless.

It is also fragile. It can be influenced by trauma, by a chemical imbalance, or by an illness. Its instincts are designed to protect the human being from danger or threats—but sometimes, that response overwhelms. Sometimes, the apprehension a person has prevents them from taking an active role in life. Sometimes, things that used to matter don't matter anymore. Sometimes, friends and family members are shut out—and being alone becomes the only choice.

Anxiety and depression are two of the most prevalent mental health diagnoses. That means that people who have these concerns don't have to feel like they are alone. Others have struggled with similar issues; others have been overwhelmed by anxiety; others have found ways to manage the symptoms as well as the disorder.

An important consideration is that anxiety disorders are not the same for everyone. Each person is triggered by something different—depending on their own life experiences and self-consciousness.

What Is Anxiety?

Expectant parents feel anxious as they anticipate the birth of their child. A spouse is anxious to hear the update from a surgeon about whether the surgery to remove a cancerous tumor went well. A high school student is anxious about stepping onto the stage to perform in the school's talent show. Passengers on an airplane feel a little anxious when turbulence is encountered.

Through the course of a day, a week, a month, a year, or even a lifetime—there will be many situations and circumstances that make a person anxious. Many of these are short-lived and cause no harm—rather, these worrisome moments assist the person in getting over fears as well as gaining confidence and experience to make it easier the next time around.

Anxiety is defined as a feeling of apprehension and fear. From a medical standpoint, these feelings of apprehension and fear are physically displayed by symptoms such as palpitations, sweating, and feelings of stress. Anxiety is a natural reaction—but if it becomes excessive, it can lead to more profound mental health issues and even impede someone from completing everyday tasks and responsibilities. This serious reaction to anxiety is considered an anxiety disorder. This mental health concern afflicts an estimated 40 million adults in the United States. That is about 18 percent of the population. Eight percent of children and teens also suffer from an anxiety disorder of some type.

Anxiety disorders include: Generalized Anxiety Disorder which is excessive, constant worrying about the daily routine; Social Anxiety Disorder which is avoidance of social interactions in fear of being negatively judged or humiliated; Panic Disorder which is a physiological reaction brought on by feelings of terror; and phobias, which are an irrational fear of an object, place, or situation.

While the types of disorders vary, there are many common symptoms. In general, a person suffering from an anxiety disorder will have an unshakable and extreme fear or worry when this level of reaction is not necessary, such as when there is no threat or danger of physical harm.

Other commonplace emotional symptoms include restlessness, irritability, heightened awareness of the possibility of danger, tenseness, and a feeling of dread. On the physical side, a person will experience an increased heart rate, sweaty skin, headaches, shortness of breath, and gastrointestinal problems.

Anxiety disorders often mimic medical disorders, such as hyperthyroidism or heart conditions. Someone who is experiencing a panic attack and is undiagnosed with an anxiety disorder may think he or she is having a heart attack because of the similarities. Experts suggest that the first professional visit should be to a medical practitioner who can rule out medical reasons for the symptoms, followed by a referral to a mental health professional for an evaluation and plan of treatment.

Because anxiety disorders have unique characteristics, the treatment plans for these conditions is individualized. Routine treatments include psychotherapy, medications, and other techniques such as learning to reduce stress and foster relaxation.

How Fear Develops into Anxiety

Doctors cite two main sources for anxiety disorders – family genetics and life experiences. Evidence suggests that anxiety disorders tend to manifest generation to generation. If a family member, such as a parent, has an anxiety disorder, the risk of their offspring developing one greatly increases.

These psychological conditions can also come about from a traumatic experience, such as the death of a loved one, a long-lasting illness, an abusive relationship or exposure to violence of any kind.

But an anxiety disorder does not materialize overnight. It is a process that moves through stages and often spans years of experiences that contribute to the irrational fear. It is like a snowball that gathers both mass and force as it travels. A single incident is not likely to result in an anxiety disorder, but repeated exposure to similar incidents put a person at risk.

While family history tends to play a role, most research also suggests secondary sources as contributing to the development of anxiety disorders. These can include brain chemistry, life events and the personality of the afflicted person.

There could also be a medical reason for the events that build the anxiety levels a person will experience. Some of the medical reasons impacting anxiety include asthma, diabetes, drug abuse, heart disease, hormones, seizures, and thyroid conditions, to name a few. The first step in seeking an answer to the symptoms occurring is to seek the advice of a medical professional who can rule out other causes for the elevated fears and apprehensions.

Anxiety can also build up over time as a result of external factors. Some of the most common environmental causes include stress at work and school, marriage or relationship challenges, money troubles, substance abuse and a lack of oxygen.

The fear or worry experienced by a person could develop into an anxiety disorder over time. As the body releases hormones and prepares to confront the fear, it slows down some body functions in order to provide support to physical needs in fending off the threat.

Consider Post Traumatic Stress Disorder as an example of how prolonged exposure to fear can develop into a serious mental health issue. In war, soldiers witness extreme acts of violence, and they are constantly on high-alert. The adrenaline and other hormones which are designed to maximize responses in dangerous situations are at a continual high level.

The impacts of this on the physical body is that it weakens the body's natural defenses to ward off infection and hinders the immune system. Stomach and intestinal problems can wreak havoc on the physical wellbeing, as well as age the body more quickly.

Long-term exposure to fear also impairs the brain's ability to store long-term memory. Damage can occur to the memory center of the brain, called the hippocampus. This causes a cyclic effect in that the brain loses the ability to submerge the fear reaction and the individual is always operating on high alert. This constant state of fear means the world around the person is wrought with danger and the memories associated with that fear confirm that assessment.

Fight or Flight of Anxiety

Humankind has always had the benefit of survival instincts to answer threats to safety or perils that may manifest. These instincts allow for two responses – flight, as in the running away from danger – or fight – facing an opponent head-on. Humans are not facing the same dangers that plagued prehistoric ancestors. The fight-or-flight response is still active in modern humankind, and it triggers physiological responses in the body in reaction to these perceived threats and dangers, whether these threating scenarios will cause bodily pain or mental anguish. In the case of anxieties and phobias, the dangers are not physical but the psychological reaction to stressors.

These instincts to get away or stay and fight is often referred to as the acute stress response. When this response is activated, the body releases hormones such as adrenaline and cortisol, among others. Other physical symptoms that display with this response an increased blood pressure, pale or flushed skin, dilated pupils and trembling. Once triggered, it could take up to an hour for the body's reactions to dissipate and functions return to normal.

The original intent of these physiological responses was to prepare the body for battle and to heighten awareness of the potential dangers. For example, while in this heightened state, the body's ability to clot blood faster is activated to reduce the loss of blood from injuries. The pupils dilate to help vision improve, and the person can focus on any nearby threats. As the body's muscles tense for the fight, trembling may occur.

While this response in the ancestors was likely triggered by an attack from a saber-tooth tiger or an attack coming from of a competing tribe, today's response may be activated by a growling dog, an annual job performance review from a boss or a sales pitch to win a multi-million-dollar contract. It could also be triggered by less threatening events, such as taking a college entrance exam or even filling out a job application. Fight-or-flight is not only triggered by a physical attack, such as a mugger or rapist, but also by psychological factors.

By priming your body for action, you are better prepared to perform under pressure. The stress created by the situation can actually be helpful, making it more likely that you will cope effectively with the threat. This type of stress can help you perform better in situations where you are under pressure to do well, such as at work or school. In cases where the threat is life-threatening, the fight-or-flight response can play a critical role in your survival. By gearing you up to fight or flee, the fight-or-flight response makes it more likely that you will survive the danger.

The body's responses in the fight or flight are controlled by the nervous system. When confronted with a real threat, such as an angry animal with claws and fangs, its good to know the body has a response to this situation. When confronted by an angry customer, choosing to fight or choosing escape would likely not result in a positive outcome. Learning to control this reaction reduces the amount of stress a person is subjected to. A constant state of stress is harmful to the body's innate defenses.

Understanding the body's reaction to stressful situations and recognizing the signs that the fight-or-flight response is being triggered is essential to learning how to manage stress. The management techniques to calm the physiological and psychological reactions to a real or perceived danger results in a healthier mind and body. Stress management, and with it the ability to calm the fight-or-flight response, is key to resolving physical, emotional and mental health concerns.

Panic Attacks

Panic is defined as a sudden uncontrollable fear or anxiety, often causing wildly unthinking behavior. There are many words to describe this, such as terror, agitation, and hysteria among others. One of the effects of severe anxiety is what health professionals call a panic attack.

It is a common occurrence. An estimated 2.4 million people suffer a panic attack each year in the United States. It usually begins when a person is in their latter part of the teenage years and early young adult stage.

This attack is a period of extreme fear that causes grave reactions by the body as if the body was responding to danger as in the fight or flight response. A person who is experiencing a panic attack may think he or she is having a heart attack, losing control of their physical and mental abilities, or even that death is near. It is a frightening experience for the individual, as well as family members or friends.

Panic attacks can happen once in a while or can be a chronic consequence of an anxiety disorder. It can also trigger another fear that another attack is imminent.

There is no way to predict when a panic attack is going to occur. That complicates the situation for the person who is experiencing it. He or she could be in the middle of an activity, such as driving a vehicle. The attack may occur when he or she is with others or when they are alone.

The sudden onset of a panic attack means there is no way to prevent one from occurring. The attack does not have to be triggered by a stressor of any kind.

Symptoms occurring as the panic attack progresses will peak quickly. The person will feel exhausted and fatigued when the attack dissipates. When the stressful or anxiety causing situation is resolved or removed, the attack will subside.

Look for these most common symptoms to determine if a person is having a panic attack. The person will feel a loss of control and a sense of doom. Their heart rate will increase, they will begin sweating profusely, and likely complain of a headache, chest pain or dizziness.

Panic attacks also involve trembling, numbness or tingling, and abdominal cramping or nausea. Hot flashes are also a common symptom as are the chills.
The good news that panic attacks on their own are not life-threatening, but it is important to seek medical advice to make sure the attacks were anxiety related and not caused by a medical condition.

Social Anxiety and the Mind

Remember the first day at a new school? Or the first day at a new job? How about going to a party at which most of the people are strangers? What happens when it's time to share an opinion on the company's new sales campaign?

All of these examples are situations in which someone who has social anxiety may have a difficult time making it through without a panic attack. Everyone gets nervous about meeting people and standing out in a crowd. Usually, those first meeting jitters give way to more confidence as the meeting and greeting conclude. Those with social anxiety, however, don't see these situations as minor moments of nervousness. For people who have been diagnosed with social anxiety disorder, these happenings are frightening and often unbearable.

Social anxiety is the fear that a person will be judged negatively by others. This fear leads the person to feel inadequate, inferior, self-conscious, embarrassed and humiliated, usually without cause. These self-deprecating thoughts seldom surface when the person is alone, only when in a social or professional setting in which attention may focus on the person.

The situations in which social anxiety may take hold of a person include being introduced to a group of people, having to say something in front of a crowd or a class or boardroom scenario. Social anxiety distress also occurs when those afflicted are teased or criticized, being watched while they do something, or when meeting influential or important people.

Social anxiety disorder, which was previously called social phobia, is estimated to affect millions of people all over the world. In the United States, studies have determined that it is the third most common psychological disorder affecting about seven percent of the population.

Like other anxiety disorders, social anxiety disorder is an extreme reaction to a fear, in this case of social disapproval. Some people have a general type of social anxiety which manifests in almost all types of human interaction, and others have a more specific variation of social anxiety, such as answering questions in class or doing oral presentations.

A person with social anxiety will react to uncomfortable situations with intense fear, and showing signs of physiological distress, including a rapid heart rate, a flushed face, dry mouth, muscle twitches and trembling.

Most people diagnosed with this disorder logically understand that their feelings are not based on fact, but simply their own perceptions. Psychologists explain that understanding that these negative thoughts about what others are thinking about him or her are different than accepting reality. Any social misstep is exaggerated by those with social anxiety, even though it may not have mattered to anyone else.

Myths About Social Anxiety

There are many misconceptions about social anxiety. Like all myths, perpetuating these falsehoods is unfair to those who have to deal with the repercussions of their disorder every day.

- Myth: Social Anxiety is the same as shyness.

It is easy to confuse social anxiety and shyness. People who are shy exhibit many of the same characteristics as those with social anxiety disorder. Shy people are uncomfortable in social situations; they are reluctant to talk to people they don't know and are not likely to voluntarily share their opinions or comments.

Those with social anxiety do not always avoid situations. In fact, anxiety occurs because they are in these situations.

Shyness could be considered a form of social anxiety. Shy people withdraw from social contact and avoid contact with others. The reasons for the shyness could be partly blamed on fear.

- Myth: Fears of public speaking are the only way social anxiety is triggered.

While a requirement to present a dissertation on some academic subject or a speech on economic development may create anxiousness and fear in the presenter, social anxiety is not limited to this narrow scenario.

Social anxiety disorder encompasses a wide range of interpersonal relationships, whether conducted in a professional or casual environment, with strangers or acquaintances. It could be a special occasion, like making a toast at a wedding or it could occur while having dinner out with friends or family.

The type of social encounter or the atmosphere has the same impact. The anxiety is a result of the fear that the person with social anxiety is being judged negatively.

- Myth: There is no solution to social anxiety other than learning to live with it.

Each person who is diagnosed with a social anxiety disorder will have a different experience. Some will have such severe responses to the thought of interacting with people that they seldom leave home or hold down a job. Others interact and be part of the community, but may have a specific fear, such as being in charge or the center of attention or possibly speaking in public.

Those with a social anxiety disorder can be helped with effective treatments. Medication is one option, and another is cognitive-behavioral therapy. With these solutions, a social anxiety disorder can be managed.

- Myth: Social anxiety is just nervousness.

Nervousness is just one of the symptoms of social anxiety disorder. It also involves physiological changes as the anxiety level increases. The capability to think, such as in engaging in small talk, is affected, as is the person's emotions.

The idea of meeting someone new isn't the cause of social anxiety; it's how that person may judge the person with social anxiety.

People are nervous when doing anything for the first time. For those with social anxiety, the distress goes above and beyond the effects of nervousness.

- Myth: Social anxiety disorder does not cause any harm to a person.

Like all forms of stress, social anxiety causes the body to react in physical, emotional and psychological ways. Elevated heart rates, rapid breathing and other physiological consequences that occur chronically can cause other medical conditions.

Stress is a serious consequence and over time can result in premature aging, loss of cognitive functions and serious medical conditions such as heart disease, diabetes, and ulcers.

When Social Anxiety Gets Serious

Unlike training for a marathon or perfecting a musical arrangement, social anxiety disorder does not get easier the more times a person experiences it. In fact, the opposite is true.

Without intervention and a plan of treatment, anxieties can compound and take its toll on work, family and social relationships. Each time social anxiety is triggered, it creates reinforces the fears that the person has about being negatively evaluated.

Continued focus on the perceived negative judgments of others causes low self-esteem, the development of poor social skills, preference for isolation, withdrawal from family and friends, and low achievement. These consequences can also lead to substance abuse and even the taking of one's life.

As social anxiety progresses, it may become increasingly difficult for the person to stay employed or stay connected with friends and family. The isolation that occurs can lead to other disorders, complicating treatment.

Social anxiety is often accompanied by other mental health disorders, such as depression. The possibility of other diagnoses compounds the serious consequences of social anxiety disorder.

It is better to seek help before the disorder becomes too ingrained in the person's lifestyle. When seeking help, provide as much information as possible to the mental health practitioner. This information can be detailed in a journal to help the person, and the practitioner determines what seems to be the predominant stressor in their daily routine.

As social anxiety progresses, it will limit the life experiences available to the person who suffers from the disorder. Pushing past the anxiety will become more difficult, and the maintenance of a normal life becomes almost impossible.

What Is a Phobia?

Everyone has their fears. Some people do not like spiders; others are afraid of snakes. One person may be scared of heights, and another person may become irrational when in the presence of a clown.

When these fears become excessive and irrational, it is called a phobia. People who have a phobia often react in the extreme when they encounter their fear. Whatever it is that triggers this fear, a phobia is specific in nature and revolves around an object, place, or situation.

A fear may cause a nervous feeling in the stomach. A phobia may cause someone to avoid a situation completely. Extreme panic reactions are also common for phobias.

Phobias are a serious disorder because it can affect that individual's daily life. It can stop them from going to work or school, it can intrude upon their personal relationships, and it can alter the way they want to live their lives. Phobias affect about 19 million people in the United States.

The causes of phobias are genetic and environmental. Someone who has experienced a trauma or witnessed a tragic event may develop a phobia. A person who may have suffered an accident in the water can develop aquaphobia. A person who was bitten by a dog in childhood may have cynophobia.

Age, gender and socioeconomic status are also risk factors in developing certain phobias. For example, men are more prone to develop phobias related to medical or dental procedures. Women are more likely to suffer from a fear of animals. Children who grow up in economically challenged households are more likely to be diagnosed with phobias related to social situations.

Phobias may also be triggered by chronic medical conditions or health concerns in general. Those who have experienced a traumatic brain injury, have substance abuse issues or have been diagnosed with depression often develop phobias.

In general, most phobias can be categorized into five distinct areas, according to the Diagnostic and Statistical Manual of Mental Disorders provided by the American Psychiatric Association. These categories are fears related to animals or insects; fears related to the natural environment; fears related to blood, injury, or medical issues; fears related to specific situations; and the "other" category which covers fears that are not related to the other four categories.

Some of the most common phobias are:
- Agoraphobia: a fear of places or situations in which the person feels trapped, such as in a crowded public place
- Acrophobia: the fear of heights
- Arachnophobia: the fear of spiders
- Astraphobia: the fear of thunder and lightning

- Autophobia: the fear of being alone
- Aviophobia: fear of flying.
- Claustrophobia: a fear of enclosed or tight spaces, such as elevators
- Dentophobia: the fear of the dentist or dental procedures.
- Glossophobia: the fear of speaking in front of an audience. It is also known as performance anxiety.
- Hemophobia: a fear of blood or injury
- Mysophobia: the fear of dirt and germs
- Nyctophobia: the fear of nighttime or the dark
- Ophidiophobia: the fear snakes

People who have phobias often experience physiological changes when confronted by what they fear. This can include an accelerated heartbeat, shortness of breath or hyperventilation, speech difficulties, and other symptoms related to panic attacks. In some cases, a person with a phobia may faint or pass out or be unable to move. Others will be moved to tears, and others get aggressive.

A common perception is that a person can overcome their phobias by confronting what it is that they fear. There is some narrative evidence that facing an object of fear can help lessen the reaction of the individual.

A mental health therapy called flooding is designed to place a patient in close proximity to their phobia. This is usually done in combination with other therapies and under the supervision of the therapist. Taking a self-help approach and using the flooding method may make the phobia worse or create a more panicked situation.

If someone responds by fleeing the scene, it could become dangerous because the reaction is to get away from the object that frightens them. If someone strikes out when frightened, others could be injured when that person reacts.

Treating a phobia is best handled by someone who has the training and experience to oversee the treatment. In most cases, it does not take very long to achieve some sort of positive result from treatment. Occasionally medications are also used in combination with therapy.

Learning ways to deal with the fear that a phobia brings on is beneficial. Instead of flooding, another way to build resistance to a phobia is desensitization, which is the gradual exposure to the object of the phobia.

Anxiety, social anxiety, and phobias are serious problems that directly impact the way people live their lives. Therapy and treatment can help reduce the reaction to situations which cause anxiety or fear. While some strategies, such as learning coping skills, can be mastered without professional guidance, it is always recommended that therapy is administered by trained professionals who have the know-how and experience to intervene if needed.

There is no common denominator, no common thread that can identify what situations will cause someone to panic or be overcome with worry and fear. Most of the time, fears are manageable. When they become life-affecting, it is time to seek help.

Chapter 2: Managing Social Anxiety

Hope is powerful, especially to someone for whom the everyday encounter of others is part of a nervous, scary, or even emotional possibility. In addition to the standard treatment offered by mental health professionals, such as therapy and or medications, there are ways for someone with social anxiety to take some level of control back by doing some homework to manage the effects of the disorder.

Part of this management rationale is to change the way the mind thinks and reacts. It is striving to change the way a person sees themselves and the inner dialogue that feeds anxiety.

Managing social anxiety means working on the individual to change the way that they view their abilities. Raising self-confidence and rewiring the brain to replace a negative point of view with a positive one can make a tremendous difference in dealing with the aggravations, fear, and emotional turmoil of anxiety.

Some of the common stressors for a person with social anxiety include public speaking or talking in public, attending parties and galas, conversing with strangers, waiting in line, using public restrooms and public transportation, and doing any activity in front of others.

Rewiring the Thinking Patterns

Social anxiety is triggered by thoughts as opposed to actions, which makes it difficult to avoid. While it is possible to remove oneself from any human interaction, that is not a healthy choice nor is it a lifestyle of value and quality. For the person with social anxiety disorder, it is the thought that he or she is being negatively judged by others, which then ultimately creates the anxiety.

One way to overcome the thoughts associated with a person's feelings of inadequacy that stems from their social anxiety disorder is to change the way the thoughts are perceived and to reinterpret the negative into a positive. Rewiring the negative thoughts with positive ones is a step forward but one that will take perseverance and training.

A daily routine of positive affirmations and challenging perceptions with reality is needed. This is not an easy fix. Unlike reconditioning the human body, reconditioning the mind is much more difficult. As muscles are toned and strengthened, there are obvious results. As changes are made in the thought patterns, people with a social anxiety disorder may not be aware of any progress being made.

One of the first thinking patterns to be challenged is that being anxious is unnatural. Anxiousness is part of the human experience. It is a throwback to the ancestors who only had their instincts to rely on. Anxiousness is the body's way of gearing up for a challenge—and it makes sure that whatever challenge may be ahead, the individual is ready to do their best.

Worrying about how others perceive each other is not uncommon. Everyone is vulnerable to feeling criticized, bullied, ignored or excluded from a group. Human beings are tribal in nature and learned interdependency to survive the trials and tribulations. People are social creatures, and group acceptance and inclusion is important.

It is important to remember that not everyone is going to find universal acceptance by every human being on the planet. People with whom there is much in common are more likely to be accepting of people who are similar themselves. Acceptance of the fact that everyone will, at times in their life, feel the sting of rejection. Accepting this can help ease the impact of those occasions when social anxiety kicks in.

Often these thought patterns are a result of genetics. Research has determined that anxiety is common through generations in a family.

Or, these thought patterns are a result of an environment in which family members were suspicious of those outside their family and social circles. Growing up in an environment in which others were inhospitably treated or were publicly judged in a supercritical and negative manner also sets in motion the idea that this treatment of others is the norm. This thought pattern could also have come from humiliating experiences either as a child or an adult.

Another way to reprocess the thinking that occurs within the mind of someone who experiences social anxiety is to change the way anxiety is perceived. For example, excitement and anticipation of something good happening mirror the same physiological effects as anxiety. People who are in love often have "butterflies" and other physical symptoms that indicate that their body is responding to anxiousness. Instead of a dialogue that focuses on being anxious, substitute excited instead.

Remember that what you think about what will happen is not reality. Human beings have a constant inner dialogue that helps them get through the day. People use these thoughts to determine a course of action to take or what to say when called on in class. These inner conversations can be helpful, but they can also be detrimental, especially for a person with social anxiety.

Instead of using this inner dialogue as reassurance of their abilities, it becomes a voice of worry and fuels any anxiety a person may be feeling. Instead of being an optimistic pep talk about the possibilities, the inner voice of a person with social anxiety disorder is predicting the worst possible outcome. Their inner voice is telling them that people won't like them, that their presentation will be rejected, or their performance publicly criticized.

To change this routine and change the dynamics between what the inner voice expects and the reality of the situation, a person must become more aware of what they are thinking and why this thought is prevailing. A journal or diary can prove helpful in understanding what sparks the negative dialogue and which situations are the most significant in fueling this anxiety.

Record not only the where's and why's about what is causing the anxiety but make an effort to record the thoughts occurring as the situation unfolds. Include any positive outcome, such as a compliment given, or a new acquaintance made, to create a positive memory of the event.

Unlike strategies which use positive thinking as a motivator, when someone with a social anxiety disorder begins looking at the situation realistically, the thought processes behind the anxiety begin to change.

Those afflicted with a social anxiety disorder can also learn to refocus the attention on how to be better prepared for the situation. When a person is anxious, his or her attention is focused on feelings and how their body is responding. Training the person to instead go over notes for a presentation or listening intently to conversations changes the direction of thoughts from inward to outward. Notice the details in the rook or the clothes a person is wearing. This change in focus diverts attention away from fears and anxiety into an awareness of the surroundings.

One technique that has helped change the way in which people with social anxiety disorders look at trigger situations is called Acceptance and Commitment Therapy. This encourages people to face their anxieties, to put up with the nervousness and uncomfortable feelings. With this therapy, clients learn to be aware of their discomfort but forge ahead anyway to keep their lives on track.

Boosting Self-Confidence

A low level of self-confidence is one of the effects that social anxiety disorder causes in a person who suffers from it. Although self-confidence and self-esteem are used interchangeably, these terms refer to very different perceptions. Self-esteem is defined as how a person values themselves. Self-confidence reflects an individual's assurance that in their own abilities to complete tasks, respond to demands and face challenges and their trust in making the right decisions and judgments.

Someone who is afflicted by social anxiety will question whether they have the abilities, talents, skills, knowledge, etc. to handle the social situation well. A student who has practiced for a speech to be given in class has memorized the content but will fear that he or she will not remember the speech, or may not have included the most important information, or that he or she may stumble over the words or mispronounce them.

The fear that somehow their abilities are not enough to protect them from ridicule or criticism is what drives social anxiety. Building confidence can quiet these fears and although the person who has a social anxiety disorder may still experience discomfort, boosting self-confidence can provide encouragement to follow through with the experience or opportunity.

Belief is one's abilities, skills, and talents make it easier to experience new things, to put one's self in situations that may be uncomfortable. It keeps a person moving forward in life, such as deciding to change careers, ask for a promotion, begin dating, or hosting a holiday party. For a person with social anxiety, these situations are fraught with fear, but improving this person's self-confidence can impact their abilities to follow through.

To improve one's belief in their abilities, there are some tips that can help.

- Don't compare yourself to others: When a person compares themselves to another person, that comparison is often based on external factors, such as occupation, annual salary, college degree, etc. Those who make these comparisons are likely to become envious of what another person has. According to research, there is a correlation between envy and a person's perceptions of themselves. Comparisons do not take into account the personal struggles, sacrifices, efforts or circumstances it took for someone to get to a particular point in their life. Assuming that everyone's path is the same is not only erroneous but detrimental to self-confidence.
- Build your confidence by putting yourself in the situations that cause you anxiety, even if it's only by role-playing with trusted friends. Ask a stranger how to get to the grocery store, introduce yourself to a fellow parent at your child's school. Each time a person makes it through these scenarios, confidence builds.

- Look for positive outcomes in every situation you experience. Acknowledge the applause you receive, respond to genuine greetings, note the smiles from people you encounter. Tallying these positive affirmations reinforces positive experiences and builds confidence that similar responses will accompany other experiences.
- Treat yourself with kindness. When a mistake is made, or something does not go as planned, consider that no one is perfect. Mistakes happen all the time to everyone. Instead of chastising yourself, roleplay how you would comfort a friend who had messed up.
- Jump in despite your doubts. When someone is unsure of how well they will do, they often forego trying. That leaves talents untapped, such as a closet singer who would be awesome in a community theater's performance of My Fair Lady or an artist's innovative technique that stays hidden from public exhibition. Prepare for the opportunity, whether that means memorizing a speech or getting better at small talk. Try out your talents in front of family and friends and practice to build confidence.
- A healthy body is a confidence builder. Eating properly, getting plenty of sleep and engaging in physical activity benefit the body and the mind. Getting exercise and staying healthy provides a positive outlook.

Managing Self-Consciousness

Self-Consciousness is simply being aware of one's self, especially to have a heightened awareness. This awareness often makes a person uncomfortable because of the perceptions a person has about themselves and how he or she believes others will see them.

Ever been called on to answer a question in class? When this happens, a person will become nervous. Instead of focusing on the answer, that person may instead be focusing on how their body is responding to being called on. Perhaps he or she begins sweating. Maybe their face gets flushed. When the focus shifts from an external point of view to an internal one, that is self-consciousness in action.

The problem with this is that for someone with a social anxiety disorder, this self-awareness often comes with negative thoughts. The person may lose focus on the question or the task and instead worry about how those around them will judge their nervousness. It can result in acting out of character or responding in a way that would not normally be an option without the onset of self-consciousness.

Self-consciousness is influenced not only be a person's own insecurities but by societal pressures as well. It no longer is simply something that happens in a face-to-face situation, but it can also occur during interaction on social media or in an online environment. Because of technology and digital access, there is no place that is safe for a person who has a social anxiety disorder. The pressure to fit into this often self-centered and narcissistic social media world is tough when a person is preoccupied with how others perceive them.

Self-consciousness is best illustrated as the voices in a person's head that repeat the negative perceptions the person has collected through their years. The insecurities, the hurt feelings, the playground comments from bullies all take a toll. These comments are stored in the memory, and when a person is experiencing self-consciousness, these memories are replayed. "You're weird. You're ugly. People are laughing at you. Don't embarrass yourself."

The list goes on and acts to remind the person of all the perceived failings in life. When self-consciousness kicks in, the fear of eliciting that same response surfaces. A person who was rejected when asking someone out on a date may carry that rejection with them, affecting their ability to ask another person out. Someone who was teased because of the way they pronounced a word, will be reluctant to speak in public. Because a person is aware of these perceptions, self-consciousness could make them respond differently in situations. Someone who is outgoing may become more introverted. A person may try harder to impress people when he or she is seeking acceptance by a group. Blending in instead of standing out may be the only option for someone whose self-consciousness is elevated.

Comments made by others about another person are not necessarily reality. But it is difficult to silence these harsh critics when a person has a high-level response to self-consciousness. The tendency to act natural or be ourselves is pushed aside; instead, a person reacts in the way they believe will shield them from criticism.

To combat the influence of this negative inner voice, a person has to identify what is damaging about these perceptions as well as how this perception became so ingrained in the mind. Once this understanding is realized, there are steps to take that can help a person overcome this destructive self-conscious state.

- Challenge self-criticism, the first step, requires the individual to identify the source of the criticism and counter the criticism with a reality-based viewpoint that is kinder and more compassionate. It calls for the development of awareness – how these inner criticisms influence a person's behavior and reactions and how this criticism detracts from the person's goals and accomplishments.

- Cut yourself some slack: Becoming your own best friend is good advice to move on past the self-consciousness. What do you admire about your friends? What are their good qualities? Take these reflections and turn the light on yourself. Learning to appreciate the individual traits, strengths, and uniqueness about ourselves is a way to counter the negative perceptions a person has stored away. Replace those critiques with self-compliments.

- Do a reality check in your head: An individual's actions, behavior, personality or appearance is always more important to themselves than to others. People who are self-conscious inflate the negative reactions they perceive about themselves and project this same reaction to those around them.

For example, a department supervisor is asked to lead a training session for his or her employees. The presentation involves policy and procedures which the department head has formulated, with the approval of management. As the presentation begins, the supervisor makes a mistake. He or she quickly catches it but has a hard time getting over the embarrassment of making a mistake in front of staff. Internally, the supervisor is thinking that the employees are smirking at his or her discomfort. The voice inside the supervisor's head may say, "You don't know what you're doing, and now everyone knows." In reality, the staff is probably not paying close attention to the presentation or have formed no opinion. In reality, most people know how difficult it is to speak in front of others and are likely glad they were not the ones who had to give this presentation.

- Lighten your mood: Remember that everyone makes mistakes and finding the humor in something that did not go as planned takes the pressure off helps a person move on. Very few mistakes or errors are as serious as a person thinks and making a joke or funny comment tips the scales toward a healthy balance.

Find strength in who you are: In the laws of physics, every action has an equal and opposite reaction. When a person steps into the spotlight, it is an act of courage. It makes that person vulnerable to feeling unworthy or judged. The vulnerability is a necessary part of finding the strengths of a person. Reading the definition of vulnerability - the quality or state of being exposed to the possibility of being attacked or harmed, either physically or emotionally – makes one question why being vulnerable is something that should be embraced to build a better self-image. Don't we want to protect ourselves from harm and attacks? Isn't that what made us doubt our abilities in the first place?

If a person weren't open to experiencing new things, that person would not become aware of what their ambitions are, what ignites the passion, and what motivates them. Experiencing new things, meeting new people, going to places never visited opens up the world and allows people to step through. Every time someone quells their fears to step into the spotlight, to be social, to put a hand out to make an acquaintance, it builds confidence. The person learns that not every foray into new territory is a negative experience.

When an individual learns who they are, they replace vulnerability with strength. Each time fears give way to courage a person finds something they do well. Setbacks, such as the negative thoughts planted in the mind by others, take extra effort to overcome. Finding out more about the individual is that extra effort to transplant the negative judgments with positive, self-affirming ones.

Practice turning negative judgments about yourself into positive ones: With a slight change in words, a negative statement can become an inspirational one. Simply making a better word choice or correcting a negative statement when it is made can start the process of what's referred to as positive self-talk.

Here are some examples of how this works. Instead of saying "I can't do this," replace that with "I'll do the best I can." Instead of "Everything is going wrong" say "One step at a time and I will handle this." Instead of saying "I'll probably make a mistake," focus on what you have done to prepare.

This technique is not something that you have to use only when anxiety kicks in. By practicing turning negative statements into positive ones, it will become second nature.

Chapter 3: Social Anxiety in Daily Life

Going to work, going to school, grocery shopping, running errands, attending a teacher-parent conference at your children's school, heading to the gym, meeting friends for dinner, and going to the movies—these are all activities that a person may do as part of their daily life. The activities are familiar ones that are done as part of a routine, at familiar locations. No problem, right?

For someone with a social anxiety disorder, any or all of these routine tasks could be debilitating and fear-inducing. Everyday life for someone who is afflicted with social anxiety disorder is not routine. There is fear about going to the wrong door at your daughter's school—anxiety that your plan to reorganize the department is not going to win the boss' approval.

Social anxiety revolving around everyday tasks causes people to withdraw. It takes people out of the world and into self-imposed isolation. Their daily life is filled with worry and self-doubt, apprehension and avoidance, and defensive posturing. All of these negative emotions zap the joy out of being an active part of the community. Instead, the person with social anxiety travels through their day—hoping he or she won't be noticed, that he or she can simply blend in.

This scenario is much more common than most people believe. In the United States, social anxiety disorder is the third most diagnosed mental health concern.
A person with social anxiety will walk through the neighborhood in fear that people are watching him or her. In the socially anxious mind, people are judging them for what they are doing wrong. Maybe their shoes don't match their suit—or maybe people will think they walk funny.

A simple task like going to the bank is fear-inducing because it means being in the presence of other people, having to answer a pleasant greeting, or not knowing what to say or how to respond when someone engages in friendly conversation. What if he or she filled the deposit slip out incorrectly? What if he or she stammers when telling the teller what they want? What if they can't figure out how to send the drive-thru container back to the teller? What judgments will others make about them?

Meeting friends for a relaxing dinner is not possible for social anxiety. There will be people they don't know in the restaurant. Even though they are with people they know, it is the opinions of those they don't know that will cause anxiety. What if he or she drops a fork and everyone looks at them? What if he or she mispronounces the name of the entrée? What if they laugh too loudly?

Someone with social anxiety will avoid making a phone call, opting instead to pay a bill online or without the need for human interaction. Without having to talk to someone, he or she protects their psyche from the negative judgments they are sure will come from a human-to-human conversation. Perhaps the customer service associate will judge him or her for not speaking clearly—or for misreading their 13-digit account number.

When it comes to interacting with someone in charge, such as a boss, a teacher, a police officer, etc., people with social anxiety often react more severely. Anyone who he or she would consider to be "better" in some way will cause the symptoms of anxiety to manifest, such as an increased heart rate, sweatiness, a flushed face, or conversely, a paling of the face. It's similar to being sent to the principal's office as a child, the feeling of fear that a person is in trouble for something they said or did.

There are techniques and helpful suggestions to help those with social anxiety get through the day. There are also therapies that are helpful in helping those with this disorder manage their anxiety.

Keeping the Mind Calm

An important technique that helps those with social anxiety is to find ways to calm the mind from the nervousness and anxiety that builds in socially stressful situations. Achieving a quiet and relaxed state of mind can counter the effects of anxiety. Practicing techniques regularly as part of a daily ritual helps prolong the calming effect these have on the mind.

Several techniques work on the theory of mindfulness, a type of meditation that connects people with their thoughts and impressions. Acceptance of anxiety is a key component in using mindfulness as a resource to overcome the source of social anxiety. Knowing that the person's thoughts and feelings are wrapped up in the anxiety and accepting that is a difficult, but essential step in the process.
Waging war between the calm of mindfulness and the fury of anxiety does not achieve any long-lasting benefits. It doesn't provide any quick or short-term relief either. Mindfulness is a process of becoming aware of your thoughts, your physiological reactions and using conscious acknowledgment and affirmations to negate the effects of the anxious mind.

For mindfulness to be effective, the person has to practice the techniques without any expectations of change. Mindfulness is not a cure for social anxiety; it is simply a way of calming down the impact of the negative thoughts. It is also understanding that the body may be restless, the mind may wander, and thoughts. Mindfulness is about paying attention to what is happening and taking care to follow through with the breathing and meditation exercises each time. It is being mindful of what your mind and body are doing and experiencing at that moment in time, not 10, 20, 30 minutes before or even a week or month ago. It is in the present, right now.

Mindfulness is designed to give the individual the power to observe their own thoughts and process these in a way that resonates. Are the thoughts that come into a mind like fish in a stream, swimming into view and swimming out of view? Are these thoughts like clouds that drift across the sky? By practicing mindfulness, the person notices patterns in how he or she responds to thoughts, why some thoughts are given more importance than others and which thoughts draw interest.

Other ways to achieve a calmer mind use cognitive therapies to change the way a person interacts with the thoughts that occur.

- Separate your identity from your thoughts: Cognitive Defusion is a type of therapy that asks the person undergoing this technique to view their thoughts as information but not as a reflection of themselves. When someone is anxious, the thoughts that occur are the result of the mind's flight or fight response. The nervousness and anxiety are a result of how the brain is communicating anticipation of danger or harm. Thoughts that accompany this response are simply words and images.

Cognitive defusion tells the anxious mind that it has a choice: it can validate or not validate the thoughts that surround social anxiety. Having a choice means the person can choose to dismiss the negative thoughts in favor of finding a solution that works for them. Thoughts are a barrier to moving on. Cognitive defusion lessens the importance of these thoughts as it applies to the individual.

- Put your thoughts into categories without bothering with the content: The advantage of this mental exercise is to allow the mind to focus on the type of thoughts that are constructive as opposed to destructive. Some thoughts require a judgment; some are based on worry; others are based on hopes, and others are based on fond memories. Why waste effort on dealing with judgmental thoughts or worrisome ones?

Categorizing the type of thoughts allows the mind to skip over those that may be anxiety-producing in favor of ones that are neutral as far as the mind is concerned.

- Time changes all things: Many of the negative thoughts a person with a social anxiety disorder has come from past unpleasant experiences. Learning to dwell in the present distances the person from remembering the person, place or event that contributed to the development of their social anxiety. That time when he failed that test in fourth grade and disappointed his parents – that was a long time ago before he graduated with honors from high school and college.

Remembering that embarrassing fourth-grade test disaster may be one of the sources for his anxiety when it comes to being tested, graded, or reviewed today.

By reiterating that a person is not the same as they were in the past, that situations faced as an adult are not the same as those they faced as a child, that the people we encounter when we have free choice as to whom we wish to associate is different than when we were forced into study groups in school. Change is not necessarily a bad thing and realizing that the changes a person has undergone have shaped them and given them perspective. How has your life experience as an adult made you better able to cope with adversity?

- Discern helpful facts from unhelpful ones: When a person looks at a situation and analyzes the facts, sometimes they focus on the one that feeds into their doubts and fears. For example, a student applying to a prestigious college may focus on the fact that only 20 percent of those that apply are selected. Thinking that he or she has a four out of five chance of making the cut is defeating. By dismissing this fact, that student can focus on completing the application requirements to present themselves in the best possible light.

Calming the mind takes an approach that addresses the validity of the thoughts that surface when a person is anxious or nervous. Calming the mind also means calming the inner dialogue and teaching the brain to use logic and reason to analyze the thought process revolving around anxiety.

Managing Anxious Thoughts

Exercises to calm the mind are a good tool to have in working towards a reduction in the effects of social anxiety. But what can be used when a person is in the middle of an anxiety episode? Thoughts related to a person's social anxiety come fast, intense and recurring. These thought patterns happen whenever anxiety or stress is present, even if none of the other symptoms manifest.

Most of the time these inner beliefs are reminders of the past, of a similar time when these same feelings surfaced, such as a time of sadness, loss, or embarrassment. But, the possibilities of what will happen in the future can also be triggered. There is no pattern to these thought patterns, but they are usually overinflated worries.

It is tough and tiring to deal with these thought patterns, especially since the thoughts come quickly when the mind is agitated. It's like the brain is running on a treadmill and cannot get off. It's more difficult to focus and effects a person's ability to complete chores and even to sleep.

Slowing down the anxious mind takes a little effort but can easily be accomplished.

- Change how you view anxious thoughts: There is no use trying to avoid anxious thoughts. Repression does not work. Instead, change the way you process these. The act of reframing these thoughts as guesses reduces their importance. When the mind considers something as a fact, it suggests that the outcome is already assured. Facts are seldom wrong, but guesses are right only some of the time, depending on the odds. Counter the negative predictions of what could happen by looking at the other side of the coin. What good can come from the situation? Use your experience to determine the most likely outcome based on what you know as fact.

This technique is called cognitive distancing. Simply put, this means that understanding a situation has to take place via several points of view. Scenarios have to be looked at, and outcomes have to be weighed, both negative and positive as well as a combination of both.

- Find a calming phrase: Adopting a mantra is a proven technique to quiet the mind in a stressful situation. According to studies, the repetition of a mantra activates the area of the brain in which self-judgment and reflection occur.

There's no science to picking out a sound, word, or phrase that will act as a mantra. It simply has to be something that will allow you to focus on the mantra instead of anxious thoughts. A favorite positive quote, saying "All is OK," or simply making a sound will work. The key is to use the same mantra every time. Practice ensures that the mantra is committed to memory and can be recalled easily when needed. Don't wait until anxiety happens to practice; make perfecting your mantra recall a daily task.

Reinforcing this mantra with a physical action, like tapping an arm, hand or leg, is also helpful in redirecting the mind away from the anxiety-caused thoughts.

- Document your apprehensions: When in the middle of a stream of anxiety-related thoughts, taking time to write down the fears and dreads allows the person the opportunity to review these concerns later. It also slows down the continual influx of anxiety-related thoughts, in essence giving the brain a chance to slow down.

There is an order to writing thoughts down because it provides a way to organize and analyze. The time it takes to finish this task calms the mind and diminishes the frenzy of the anxiety-related thoughts. A calmer approach to the fears opens up the door to better reactions.

- Take a break and change the scenery: When the mind continues to focus on the same anxious thoughts, it leaves little opportunity for finding a solution to the dilemma. Standing up, stretching the body, moving to another area, or focusing on a task or activity changes a person's perspective.

An author who is struggling with writer's block may abandon his or her story for a half-hour, an hour or even a day or two. The time away from work allows the author to see things differently. It is easier to spot errors and to find a new approach to the part of the story that was proving difficult.

When someone is having anxious thoughts, turning around or moving to another area can have the same effect. A change in scenery changes the focus and provides perspective.

- Ditch the telephoto view: When a person is experiencing distress because of anxiety, the focus is on the stressor. Limiting the focus on what is causing the anxiety feeds that nervousness. The mind wants to focus on the perceived threat instead of on the complete picture.

Taking a step back to consider more than what is activating the anxiety slows down the rapid rehashing of worry and fear. Just like looking through a microscope, things look bigger than they are in real life. This holds true in reference to anxious thoughts. Giving too much importance to the anxiety makes the person miss other details about the experience.

Managing the Panic Mind

When someone is in the throes of a panic attack, there are various techniques that can be used to counter the physical effects. But what about the mind? How does someone stop the panic from affecting their thoughts and bringing about a calmer demeanor?

In addition to the worry caused by the reaction to the anxiety, during a panic attack, the mind's reaction is to add more fear and doubt. The symptoms of a panic attack mirror those of a heart attack, so one of the worries experienced by those who are having a panic attack is if they are going to die.

Because the thoughts race into the mind so quickly in this situation, finding a way to distract the mind by focusing on something else is one suggestion that helps slow down the thoughts, however, a panic attack is fear multiplied by 10. The instinct is to fight the rollercoaster of thoughts and to force the mind to focus on something else.

Instead, experts advise to wait it out. Let the thoughts race but consider it to be like a wave. During childbirth, women will experience pain in waves based on their contractions. Some of these sensations are strong and almost intolerable, and others cause discomfort. Natural childbirth classes teach techniques that help mothers make it through the toughest parts of the birthing process.

Looking at the waves of thoughts that flood the mind during a panic attack as simply a wave on the beach helps alleviate further panic.

Waves on the shore come in a regular flow, although some are bigger and others smaller. Let your mind experience the thoughts with the reassurance that it will pass.

Distract the mind with the sense of touch. Holding an ice cube in one hand and the other takes the mind's focus off the anxious thoughts. It forces the mind to settle on something in the real world instead of inside the brain. The coldness and irritation from the ice cube snap the brain from panicked thoughts to focus on the discomfort.

Thoughts can also be distracted by doing an activity that requires physical movement or the use of higher brain skills, such as solving a Sudoku puzzle or folding laundry. Because the mind has to concentrate on a task, there is less room to process negative thoughts.

Utilize reason and logic to provide alternative thoughts. Panic attacks originate with the emotions. Reason and logic come from a different part of the brain. Because anxiety and panic are so frightening, it's as if the emotions take control and every other brain functions take a back seat.

Finding a way to engage reason and logic takes control back from the emotions. It redistributes brain power across the whole spectrum instead of focusing exclusively on fear and worry.

Overcoming Panic Attacks

The sudden onset of a panic attack can be frightening. Both the body and the mind are affected when these attacks happen, which can be at any time, even while asleep.

Common symptoms include a fast heart rate, breathing difficulties, a sense of terror, a faint or dizzy feeling, chest pains, tingling or numbness in fingers and hands, sweating or chilled, and an overall feeling that the person has lost control. Panic attacks do not last a long time – most are over in 10 minutes – but it does take longer to recover from some of the symptoms.

Much of the focus on overcoming some of the symptoms of a panic attack involves getting the body to slow down its reactions. Proper breathing techniques in the height of the panic attack are an essential skill that can be used to quell anxiety and minimize stress. Those having a panic attack frequently say it is difficult to catch their breath. Common complaints from those having an attack liken it to a sense of choking, smothering or suffocating.

When a person complains that they are unable to catch their breath, it means they are not getting enough air. During a panic attack, breaths become faster, but the quality of the breathing is shallow. This means that not enough oxygen is being taken into the body and, conversely, too much carbon dioxide is being exhaled. The body needs to maintain a steady level of carbon dioxide to avoid symptoms such as a dry mouth, numbness or tingling, and chest pain caused by the tightening of the chest muscles.

This shortness of breath is also called hyperventilation and is characterized by short, shallow breaths. The danger of hyperventilation is that it can lead to faintness, light-headedness, and confusion.

A sign of someone who may be hyperventilating is the taking of short, quick breaths. Others may cough or exhibit rapid breathing.

The first step is to calm down. Not being able to breathe properly is a scary experience and is likely to cause additional panic.

Experts recommend that a person take slow and deep breaths to ease anxiety. The key to deep breathing is to remember to inhale and exhale at the same pace. To help regulate your breathing, pretend that you are blowing up a balloon.

This is a skill that can be practiced, as the ideal breath should come from the abdomen. Breathe in through the nose for a count of four and then breathe out to the same four-count rhythm. When done correctly, the abdomen should rise, and the chest should remain still.

An alternative to deep breathing is to breathe at a slower pace than your body wants to. During a panic attack, taking breaths at a slower pace puts you in better control of your breathing, and it slows down the heart. This technique is a calming influence on the flight-or-fight response.

As you breathe during a panic attack, parts of the body may tense up. Areas that are most prone to that happening are the jaw, lips, and shoulders. Try relaxing these muscles and see if the breathing improves.

Managing Stress Levels

Everyone, not just those with a social anxiety order or another phobia, has to deal with stress. Stress management is an important health concern. It affects the mind and the body and can lead to serious health issues.

Some stress is easier to handle, as the hassles of traffic jams or an extra tight deadline at the office. Other interactions, like the illness of a family member, the loss of a job, or the death of a loved one add enormous amounts of stress to the usual load.

For someone with social anxiety, managing stress becomes increasingly important to offset the times when the disorder becomes triggered, or in the case of a panic attack.

To expand on the helpfulness of a breathing technique like the one used to minimize the effects of hyperventilation during a panic attack can be especially useful. When linked to another stress reduction method, meditation, the combination has proven to be successful at calming and relaxing the body and mind.

Guided relaxations, meditation, and yoga all use variations of breathing techniques to regulate how the practitioner breaths. In all of these three programs, the goal is to become aware of the body and its functions, including how to draw a breath and how to use this natural and essential bodily function to reduce stress.

Meditation does not have to be an elaborate process. It could involve writing in a journal, indulging in art, even taking up the popular coloring books for adults. While you are involved in any activity that helps you relax and stem the constant flow of worrisome thoughts, focus on the task. It can also be a time to repeat positive, uplifting messages.

There are also scenarios that can help put the brain in the right state of mind. Remembering a special place in a person's life that has happy or relaxing memories is a way to personalize the stress management ritual.

Others may envision their stress triggers moving like the wind in all of its incarnations – a breeze, a gust, a blustery force, or even a storm. Whatever the wind does, the practitioner lets it happen in their mind, holding on to the knowledge that their calmness protects against the unpredictability.

Visualizing being at the ocean is also a common meditation scenario. In this example, the body is caressed by the sun and the sea, and tranquility comes from the rhythmic lull of the waves on the shore. Drawing parallels between the sea and one's life add another dimension to the meditation, serving as an illustrative mechanism to take charge and embrace change.

No matter the relaxation scenario a person chooses, meditation is more than simply imagining yourself in that place. It is about making observations about your meditation spot and determining how the symbolism relates to you. Meditation is learning to delve deeper into our minds and bodies to reduce worry and find inner peace. A peaceful person is happier, healthier and more resistant to stress.

Getting active is another way to reduce stress. A routine visit to the gym, a hike in the woods, or a jog around the park are all activities that produce endorphins to counteract those hormones released during stressful times.

In this technologically connected world, there are options to help people keep track of vitals like heart rate, pulse rate, oxygen levels, and calories expended. These apps are helpful for those who want to keep track of their progress.

Experts suggest several ways to stop stress quickly. These suggestions can be used individually or combined as needed.

- Take time to make a decision about something that is troubling you.
- Recite the alphabet or count to 10 before responding
- Go for a short walk away from the event, the person, or the situation that is causing you to worry.
- Listen to your favorite music, pick up your favorite book or indulge in your passion.
- Spend time with your family, friends, children or pets.
- Dissect a problem into steps and handle one at a time.

Stress Inoculation Training – A Treatment for Social Anxiety

Stress often takes a person without notice. The boss makes significant changes to the internal memo two hours before it is scheduled to be distributed. A parent gets a call that their child suffered an injury during an athletic competition. These are situations which cannot be planned, and the uncertainty is what makes it stressful.

Stress Inoculation Therapy (SIT) is a way of preparing for stressful situations beforehand by training the brain how to react when stress and anxiety occurs. Relaxation and breathing exercise play a role. Those involved in SIT learn to seek a private place to diffuse the anxiety by using coping thoughts. These abilities come from learning about stress and situations which cause stress and crafting the steps they need to take to counteract the negative effects.

For those who have a social anxiety disorder, SIT develops a plan to follow when social anxiety begins to manifest. This plan is developed by anticipating what situations cause the anxiety as well as how the individual typically responds.

SIT's philosophy is that by training a person to anticipate the consequences of a situation that person is "inoculated," or protected to a certain extent from the results of enduring the stressful situation or the social anxiety. A repercussion of repeated exposure to high-stress situations is post-traumatic stress disorder.

SIT has three phases. The first is the conceptual phase. In this phase, the person learns the basics of stress - what it is, how it happens and how it can affect the person. It also delves into how some techniques can have a negative effect when used to manage stress and reinforces effective coping skills. It is in this phase that the person will chart the stressors and how they respond to these. This information is used to fine tune the coping ideas for the individual.

The beginning stages of SIT is used to identify ongoing stressors, something that happens on a regular basis, or a time-limited stressor like a court appearance for a divorce. Every person will have their own list of stressful situations that can benefit from SIT. The training is adaptive to the individual.

The next phase is the skills acquisition and consolidation phase. During this phase, the individual is taught stress management skills developed for the individual according to their plan. These skills include cognitive restructuring, problem-solving, relaxation training, and emotional self-regulation. With these new skills, when the individual is faced with a stressful situation, he or she has options in how to respond.

Finally, the individual enters the application and follow-through phase. This is the time when the skills are put to the test, and the person faces escalating stressors, also known as systematic desensitization. By training the person to become more equipped to handle stressful situations, SIT builds confidence. The person has better self-control and enhances their abilities to reduce the harmful effects of stress.

Chapter 4: Understanding Depression

Depression is a misunderstood mental health issue. Most people equate depression with feeling sad, but it is a lot more than simply being sad, which is a real emotion that everyone experiences from time to time.

Depression goes beyond emotion. It is recognized as an illness by health experts, and every person's bout with depression is not the same as someone else's. There are treatments for depression.

There are several disorders that are classified as a type of depression.

Severe symptoms that cause the person to be unable to work, sleep, eat, or do other ordinary lifestyle tasks is characteristic of major depression. This type of depression can occur multiple times.

A persistent depressive disorder is used to classify a depression with a minimum of two-year duration. The person diagnosed with this disorder is likely to have a combination of major depressive incidents as well as periodic symptoms.

Psychotic depression is a depression that is combined with another psychosis, such as delusions or hallucinations.

Postpartum depression afflicts new mothers. An estimated 10 to 15 percent of women who give birth experience the hormonal and physical effects of this type of depression.

Some people are acutely affected by the seasons, with depression manifesting in the wintertime. This form of depression is called Seasonal Affective Disorder and is triggered by a lack of natural sunlight. Symptoms usually go away in spring. According to statistics, five percent of the population in the United States has seasonal affective disorders—with women making up 80 percent of these diagnoses.

According to statistics, women are more likely to be diagnosed with depression. Likely due, in part, to postpartum depression, women tend to have symptoms relating to sadness, feeling guilty, and worthlessness. Men, on the other hand, are more likely to have symptoms related to fatigue, difficulty sleeping, and loss of interest in activities they once enjoyed.

Children can develop depression in their pre-pubescent years—with occurrences equally distributed between boys and girls. Teens and young adults who show one or more symptoms of depression should be checked out by medical and mental health practitioners. Teenage years are difficult, and stress from school demands and peer influences are higher than at other ages. A child or teen who has been diagnosed with depression will continue to be afflicted into their adult years.

According to statistics compiled by the World Health Organization, an estimated 300 million people worldwide are afflicted with depression. In the United States, 16.2 million adults or 6.7 percent of the population have experienced a problem with depression within a 12-month period.

What Is Depression?

Depression is a life-changing illness that takes its toll on how people live their lives and interact with others. Clinical depression is the official name for the disorder that can show up in a multitude of symptoms.

A person who is depressed creates a difficult dynamic for family and friends. Not only does the depressed person feel the stress of the disorder, but their condition adds stress to family members, too. To offset this, family members are encouraged to take an active role in the diagnosis and treatment of their loved one. Counseling or therapy for the family is also an option.

As an illness, depression requires treatment. It is not something that will cure itself with the passage of time, nor can someone make themselves get better simply by willing it to be so.

Although the symptoms vary, there are some indicators that a person may be suffering from depression. If the signs do not go away in two weeks, health experts suggest that the person may be clinically depressed.

It is important to note that not everyone experiences the same symptoms or combinations of symptoms. People who are diagnosed with depression may experience different levels of severity. For one person, difficulty concentrating may be very severe, and in another, the severest symptom may be appetite changes. Some people struggle with more than a few symptoms, and others experience multiple symptoms.

These signs and symptoms include:

- Persistent sad, anxious, or "empty" mood
- Feelings of guilt, worthlessness, helplessness
- Feelings of hopelessness, pessimism
- Difficulty concentrating, remembering, making decisions
- Decreased energy, fatigue, being "slowed down"
- Difficulty sleeping, early-morning awakening, or oversleeping
- Appetite and/or weight changes
- Restlessness, irritability
- Loss of interest or pleasure in hobbies and activities
- Persistent physical symptoms
- Thoughts of death or suicide, suicide attempts

One particular group of people who are susceptible to developing depression are the elderly. This group presents a challenge because many of the symptoms of depression in younger people are different from those that manifest in older people. Medical diagnoses and prescription side effects are also considerations when determining whether a senior citizen is dealing with depression.

Common symptoms for this age group include feeling tired, being grumpy or irritable. They may have difficulty going to sleep.

Confusion is another common symptom, which is also indicative of Alzheimer's Disease, which complicates diagnoses.

On important fact about depression is that it can be treated. As with many disorders, early detection and intervention achieve better results. Medication and therapy are the most common treatment methods, either individually or in combination.

There are many misconceptions about depression that continue to add a stigma to discussions about the disorder. Depression is not sadness nor is it considered a weakness of some kind. It is a diagnosable condition with symptoms and conventional treatment options. It is caused by genetic, biological and psychological factors.

Someone who has depression cannot will themselves out of it. There is no switch that turns it on or turns it off. Changing attitudes or flooding your environment with cheerful thoughts and happy unicorns and rainbows is not a treatment. It has very little to do with grief or sadness and more to do with physiological and psychological reasons.

A tragic incident by itself does not cause depression. Grief over the death of a loved one or the ending of a relationship puts someone at risk of developing depression, but a single incident is not the cause. Depression can manifest when times are good or when times are tough, and it can be part of an ongoing period of lost hope, being withdrawn or loss of interest. Suicide is also a possibility during a depression.

How is it formed?

Like many mental illnesses, depression can be caused by a number of factors.

Genetics is one of the factors that can determine whether a person is at risk for depression. An individual who has family members diagnosed with depression is more likely to develop the disorder as well.

The genes that are part of the makeup of every human being have an effect on mood and personality. If there is a malfunction in the genes, it can change the way people respond, including affecting mood. When the genes are not on target as far as mood is concerned, any situation, event or inconvenience may trigger anxiety and stress.

Brain chemistry and other factors relating to the way the brain functions are also linked to the onset of depression. Research suggests that the chemicals inside the brain of those with depression work differently than that of non-depressed individuals. Hormone imbalances also can lead to depression. Most vulnerable to a hormone-related cause of depression are women who are undergoing a pregnancy or entering menopause.

While a direct correlation between brain chemistry and depression has yet to be formalized, research notes that there is a connection between changes in the brain and the onset of depression. Whether those changes are a result of faulty synapses or caused by elevated levels of hormones produced in stressful situations, a cause of depression is likely linked to the brain.

Trauma, grief or stress are just some of the environmental and life-experience related reasons that depression can manifest. Research also indicates that depression related to trauma does not have to have happened directly to the person that has depression. A person who witnesses tragedy can also become depressed because of it.

Seeing an event unfold such as the terrorist attack on the Twin Towers in New York on 9/11 or school shootings often shatter preconceived notions about how the world works, according to psychologists. This can lead to a panic disorder, which can develop into depression.

Depression begins most often in a person's teenage years into their 20s and 30s. High levels of anxiety in childhood have also been shown to possibly lead to depression later in life.

When depression happens alongside other serious medical diagnoses, such as cancer or Parkinson's disease, it can make conditions worse. Part of the reason this occurs can be linked to the medications used to treat these diseases, a side effect of the prescription drugs.

Depression in the Mind

Depression is a mental health disorder, and the effects of it are related to how the disorder affects brain function. The levels of cortisol, which is regulated by parts of the brain, are indicative of the brain's role in the onset of depression. As an example of this connection, researchers found that the cortisol levels for someone with depression remain high throughout the day as compared to a non-depressed person. Normal brain function records the highest levels of cortisol in the morning and decreases at night.

Science has identified three areas of the brain that are most likely involved in depression. These three have been identified as the hippocampus, amygdala and the prefrontal cortex.

The hippocampus is the memory center of the brain. Located near the center of the brain, one of its primary functions is to produce cortisol. This hormone is released when the flight-or-fight response is activated or simply in times of stress, whether that stress is physical or mental related, and when a person is suffering from depression.

While this hormone is essential as a mechanism to cope with stress when there is too much cortisol produced during stressful events or because of a chemical imbalance, are sent to the brain due to a stressful event or a chemical imbalance in the body. These high levels impact the hippocampus' ability to generate new brain cells. When someone with depression has high levels of cortisol, memory problems are a possibility.

At the front of the brain is the prefrontal cortex. This area of the brain is affected by high levels of cortisol, impacting its abilities to regulate emotions, form memories and assist in a person's decision-making abilities. Too much cortisol has been shown to shrink the prefrontal cortex.

The third part of the brain, the amygdala becomes enlarged when a person has depression due to the high levels of cortisol produced in the hippocampus. The function of this area of the brain is to prompt the appropriate emotional response, such as fear, feelings of happiness or pleasure. When this area of the brain is impacted, sleep will be disrupted, and the usual activity patterns of the individual will also be altered. In additional complication, an impacted amygdala can trigger the release of hormones and chemicals in the body.

When the amount of cortisol as well as other elements in brain chemistry is balanced, shrinkage of the hippocampus occurs. Achieving this balance can address memory problems and reduce the symptoms of depression.

To do this, medication is a common treatment. Several prescription medications are successful in balancing brain chemistry. Some of the most commonly prescribed are:

- Selective Serotonin Uptake Inhibitors (SSRI)
- Serotonin-Norepinephrine Reuptake Inhibitors (SNRI) and Tricyclic Antidepressants:
- Norepinephrine-Dopamine Reuptake Inhibitors (NDRIs)
- Monoamine Oxidase Inhibitors (MAOI)

Serotonin, norepinephrine, and dopamine improve both energy and mood levels, as well as act on brain cell communication. The following pharmaceutical classification allows the body to relax, thus suppressing brain cell communication and slowing down the production and release of cortisol.

- Atypical Antidepressants: Included in this group are mood stabilizers, tranquilizers, and antipsychotics.

Therapy is also an option in helping to restore brain function. Some examples of the therapy often used to correct the brain chemistry imbalances are:

- Electroconvulsive therapy (ECT) – to improve brain cell communication, electrical current is passed through the brain.

- Transcranial magnetic stimulation (TMS) – targets the brain's ability to regulate mood by directing electric pulses into the cells of the brain charged with this function.

The third method of that has shown some success in research is psychotherapy. The definition of psychotherapy is simply therapy which occurs between an individual and a trained mental health therapist in which psychological issues are examined. It is believed that therapy sessions like this relieve depression symptoms and help change the way in which the prefrontal cortex part of the brain responds.

In addition, doctors often recommend that a person suffering from depression can also make healthy choices, especially those that directly impact brain health. These healthy choices include eating nutritional foods and pursuing an active lifestyle, both of which boost brain cell communication. Getting plenty of sleep is found to grow brain cells as well as repair damaged cells.

Suicide – Myths of Suicide

About 41,000 people committed suicide in a single year. An estimated 1.3 million adults have attempted suicide, and 2.7 adults have voiced the intention to commit suicide. Mental health researchers estimate that 9.3 million adults have suicidal thought.

Statistics indicate that women are more likely to attempt suicide, but men are more likely to die from suicide.

Suicidal thoughts are a serious consequence of depression. About half of those who attempt suicide have been diagnosed with a mental health disorder. What prevents many people from seeking help are some of the misinformation that surrounds suicide and suicidal thoughts.

For the rest of those who attempt or commit suicide, the self-destructive tendency is prompted by a number of stress factors occurring in a person's life. These could be related to relationships, trouble with the law, financial problems, death of someone close, trauma, abuse, dealing with a devastating illness and other situations which cause high levels of stress and are deeply emotional to the person.

As with many other health conditions, there are some risk factors for suicide. These include: someone who has attempted suicide in the past; someone who has experienced a stressful life event; someone with a substance abuse problem; someone who has a mental health disorder; has mental health issues that run in the family; someone who has a medical condition linked to depression; and someone who is lesbian, gay, bisexual or transgender without family support.

Suicide can be prevented. Intervention by someone if a person is showing any of the warning signs can literally save a life.

If anyone is considering suicide, reach out for help. Speak to a family member or close friend. Contact a member of the faith community to talk about your feelings and thoughts. Make an appointment with your doctor.

Call 911 or a local emergency number. Call a hotline to speak with someone who can help. The National Suicide Prevention Lifeline is 1-800-273 TALK. Veterans can also call that number and press "1."

- **Myth: A suicidal person will always be suicidal.**

Research indicates that suicidal intentions are short-term and are usually situation-specific. With proper treatment, these thoughts and intentions can be controlled.

People consider suicide when they are dealing with powerful emotions and deeply wounding thoughts that are not being controlled. If the thoughts are managed and lose their intensity, the idea of committing suicide goes away.

- Myth: Most suicides happen without warning.

Individuals who are entertaining thoughts of suicide often exhibit warning signs, either verbally or in the way that person is behaving.

Sometimes these warning signs are observed by those the person feels closest too. Outside of family and friends, these thoughts, and behaviors are kept secret.

Although warning signs don't come highlighted or with a flashing light to draw someone's attention, there are signals that often point to a person's suicidal state of mind. Warning signs of suicide include:

✓ Avoiding and withdrawing from contact with family and friends and expressing the desire to be left alone
✓ Extreme mood swings, from very happy and optimistic to very sad and pessimistic, in a matter of hours

✓ Talking about killing themselves or expressing, "I wish I were dead," or similar comments.

✓ A preoccupation with violence, death and dying

✓ Increased substance abuse

✓ Increased risky or dangerous behavior

✓ A change in sleeping or eating patterns

✓ Taking steps to acquire the means to end a life

✓ Giving away belongings or putting affairs in order when there appears to be no reason

✓ Expressing a feeling of being trapped or hopeless in a situation

• Myth: Suicide is a result of depression.

When the numbers of people who are diagnosed with depression are compared with the number of people who commit suicide, it becomes obvious that this myth is untrue. Many people who are clinically depressed do not attempt or commit suicide.

It is estimated that about half of those who die from suicide were also depressed and may also have had other psychological disorders.

While suicide is a consequence of depression, it is not the only consequence.

- Myth: Suicides are not something that can be stopped.

Evidence suggests that prevention efforts make a difference and results in the savings of countless lives every day. People who are suicidal or those who talk about suicide are sending out signals about the seriousness of their mental state. These signals are some of the warning signs that others need to cue in on.

When these warning signs are heeded, it is possible to stop someone from taking their life. Early indications that symptoms are compounding should be the call for action.

Suicide often happens as a response to the difficulties adding up.

- Myth: Talking about suicide encourages suicide.

Suicide is seldom talked about because it carries a stigma, but this topic needs to be given a voice. When suicide is discussed, it lessens the stigma and provides a way for people to seek help.

Especially when suicide is discussed on a clinical level, people who may be contemplating suicide are provided with options, facts, and resources to allow them to seek the help they need. Talking about suicide doesn't encourage it; it prevents it.

- Myth: Suicide doesn't happen to young children.

Each year about 30 children in the United States under the age of 12 commit suicide. The research on this occurrence is still incomplete, but it does happen. Prevention efforts are not typically targeting this age group.

- Myth: The act of suicide is an impulsive one.

Suicide is actually most often a planned act. The person who is considering suicide will have given it much thought, hinted at their intentions, and planned out the act, perhaps even writing final letters to loved ones. It may take as short as several days to a few weeks to reach the point in which a suicide occurs.

Suicides among children, however, are more impulsive, but there will still be signs. Perhaps the child has told a friend, discussed suicide in school work or dropped hints to an adult at school.

- Myth: Suicide is an easy way out.

According to mental health experts, people are wrong to think that suicide is all about ending life. It is a solution to ending a person's pain. The feeling of hopelessness caused by the mental anguish and the deeply emotional state the person is under is the motivation for considering suicide. People who are suicidal also feel helpless in finding a solution to relieve their emotional state.

These individuals are in a troubled mental health state. Their decision making is compromised because of the huge emotional burden they carry.

The best way to dispel the myths about suicide is to talk about it. Confronting falsehoods about this mental health issue is the best way to make sure that those who need help are poised to receive it.

What Happens When Depression Gets Serious?

There is no doubt that suicide is a serious consequence of depression. There are treatment options that can help. Clinical depression that does not get treated has serious consequences. It increases the probability of substance abuse and drug addiction, can interfere with relationships and the ability to work.

It also puts the physical body at risk. Evidence suggests that depression can impede a heart attack or stroke survivors' ability to make health care decisions, follow treatment protocol and coping with the challenges of recovery. A study also found that a heart patient with depression has a more likely chance of dying within the first few months after suffering a heart attack.

Untreated depression also manifests strongly in men. In these cases, men tend to demonstrate more rage and frustration. They may become more violent with women. They often take risks that are dangerous, such as unsafe sex, driving recklessly and other potentially life-threatening actions.

Depression is considered a disability because it seriously affects the way people live their lives. Job performance, family life and even social interactions with friends are impacted when someone is in a depressed state. Statistics indicate that sick days lost from work because of untreated depression cost more than $43 billion in costs, with 200 million-plus days of work lost.

When dealing with a family member who has depression, especially a child or teen, the parent should offer support on an emotional level. Patience, encouragement, and understanding are key to helping a family member cope with the emotional toll of depression.

Conversations should be meaningful, and not necessarily about depression. Listen carefully to what the family member or friend is saying. It is important to offer a perspective on reality as well as hope without disregarding the depressed person's feelings. Remind them that depression will prolong life, with treatment and as time goes on.

Some comments require immediate attention, like those that express a desire to hurt themselves or others and those that reference suicide.

Addiction is another possible outcome when depression is untreated. Ignoring the symptoms of depression is not a treatment option. Lack of a treatment plan to combat the symptoms of depression often leaves those exhibiting the symptoms to turn to self-medicating with drugs or alcohol. Besides the risk of developing an addiction, drugs and alcohol can make the symptoms even more pronounced.

Self-harm is another example of how untreated depression can develop into a serious consequence. Although the intention of self-harm is not to severely injure or cause death, cutting and burning can go wrong. Accidents happen, and death can occur.

Taking chances that are dangerous or reckless are also more likely to happen if the symptoms of depression are not addressed. Feelings of low self-worth, hopelessness, and anger often influence depressed people to make poor choices.

Chapter 5: Managing Depression

Depression is a serious condition that requires treatment to alleviate the symptoms and keep the disorder from becoming more serious. In addition to medical and therapeutic intervention, there are numerous ways to keep the symptoms of depression from impacting your life more than necessary.

Any illness or affliction can be helped with some non-clinical methods—such as finding the right combination of diet, sleep, and physical activity that improve brain and body function, balance psychological and physiological imbalances, and help repair damaged cells.

Like any type of management program, a planned approach is necessary, and a commitment to work the program as needed is essential. Especially when dealing with a disorder that can impact daily life and social interactions, developing a routine of positive actions can make a difference.

Many of the ways to manage depression are beneficial in reducing stress. Stressful situations stimulate the body to release higher levels of cortisol and other hormones needed in response to the body's defensive mechanisms. Controlling the levels of stress as much as possible will lead to an overall improved brain chemistry balance.

Boost Your Self-Esteem

People struggling with depression or other disorders like social anxiety have been found to have low self-esteem, self-confidence, and a heightened sense of self-consciousness. Improving self-esteem is an all-around good idea. Research has shown that people who have confidence and a high regard for their sense of self tend to be healthier and more successful.

This is a critical world. The immediate gratification found in social media means that people don't often censor themselves when it comes to leaving negative reviews or even when insults are directed at others. No one likes to be insulted or criticized—but in the end, the most important opinion is the one we have of ourselves. And sometimes, a person is harder on themselves than on another person.

Self-esteem building is a difficult task—mostly because a person has to learn to silence the internal critic and avoid comparing themselves to others. For someone who is already experiencing anxiety about what others think about them, the inner voice that feeds these fears is the enemy. Luckily, there are experts who have come up with some ways to allow a person to take control and work on improving their self-esteem.

Gaining the ability to recognize negative thoughts as simply a thought and not irrefutable proof of inabilities is a key element in being mindful. Trying to ignore the judgmental inner voice does not adequately address the situation. Being aware of how the thoughts affect the self-esteem, recognizing that these thoughts are not facts, and learning when the rationale is needed to confront the negative and substitute the positive.

What a person believes is true about their life becomes the narrative they recite and forms the judgments they make about themselves. If that narrative is one-sided, it dictates the direction of self-esteem. A positive narrative automatically raises the person's self-worth, while a negative storyline allows negative thoughts to have the most influence. To change this dynamic, a person needs to change the story.

Experts say that a person learns to communicate the negative thoughts about themselves and that replacing these with positive ones can change the inner conversation. What was once learned can be unlearned, or at least that knowledge can be replaced with a better and positive affirmation.

Affirmations are a way to replace the negative viewpoint with one that reflects the truth about ourselves. One way to zero in on the best qualities and skills is for an individual to make a list of the positive elements in his or her life, especially those that he or she possesses.

Giving this a time limit forces the brain to focus on qualities that represent the positive.

In addition to the list providing information to begin changing self-criticism, it also serves as a tool for reducing the effect of some symptoms of depression.

Rekindling interest in what makes a person happy is a way to invigorate a person's self-esteem. Identifying the activities or skills a person does well is a balance to the things that they do not do well. For example, some people are great at fixing things, such as computers, but they may not be able to sing. Someone may be a fantastic photographer but can't play tennis. It is important to remember that no one does everything well. Everyone has strengths and weaknesses.

Volunteering or engaging in charitable work is also a way to rev up self-esteem. When a person devotes time and energy to help others, the focus is no longer on themselves, but on the difference, their efforts are making in other people's lives. Lending a hand to help those less fortunate generates a good feeling, one that affirms the goodness within.

The pay-it-forward initiative is an example of how one kind act can have a ripple effect on others. When a person does something nice for another person, it creates a sense of satisfaction and accomplishment, generating a positive response in the emotion center of the brain.

Don't underestimate the power of forgiveness. Learning to forgive and let go is a way to discard the negative memories that weigh down a person's mood. Research suggests that granting forgiveness to those who been hurtful affects self-esteem. Doing so allows us to accept the shortcomings of others, generates a more loving nature and provides closure needed to move on.

The Healthy Brain (SEEDS)

There is evidence that maintaining a healthy brain can provide a way to keep depression and other anxiety disorders from becoming too severe. In terms of increasing brain health and improving cognitive awareness and function, taking an all-encompassing approach to whole body health has been a successful program for people suffering from age-related degenerative diseases, such as Alzheimer's disease.

According to research, a focus on maintaining a healthy mind improves the body's health as well and lessens the possibility of developing cognitive problems later in life. A program with the acronym SEEDS has been used with Alzheimer patients. SEEDS is Sleep, Eat, Exercise, Domain, and Social Engagement.

Individually, any of these five components are healthy for the mind and body.

Sleep gives the brain time to cleanse itself of toxins.

Healthy food choices and intermittent fasting keep the body's metabolic functions functioning well, providing nutrients to the organs and the brain.

Physical activity keeps muscles and joints fluid and releases hormones that contribute to brain and body health.

Maintaining a toxin-free living space reduces contamination and limits exposure to toxins that may be detrimental to the brain and body.

And finally, being socially active helps boost spirits and elevate mood.

Socialization

One of the symptoms of depression is a withdrawal from social situations. Sometimes depression results in isolation from friends, family, and people in general. The opportunities to interact with others become limited by depression, especially when the disorder keeps a person from going to work, attending school or visiting with other people. Interacting with others can be stressful, but it makes sense that adding a socializing element to depression management works.

People who are struggling with depression often avoid contact with people they know and people to whom they are close. They avoid doing things that were once enjoyed with others. As it worsens, people will avoid any contact with other people, including not answering the phone or returning phone calls.

Much of this avoidance comes out of fear that friends or family will judge them or that the symptoms of depression may be too much to handle for those who know and love you. The thought of meeting new people when a person is overwhelmed with debilitating emotions is not a consideration.

To keep depression from getting to the point where a person becomes isolated, making an effort to mingle with others, have a conversation, or experience a shared interest is an effective way to minimize the progression of symptoms. Studies indicate that people who socialize are less likely to become depressed and those who distance themselves from social contact are at risk of becoming depressed.

People who have been diagnosed with depression or social anxiety feel alone in their struggle. That feeling is compounded by the lack of contact with others. Being alone feels unnatural to the human psyche, based on the communal lifestyle of the human experience.

Besides lessening loneliness, socialization draws a person out of their focus on their problems and worries. Sharing the experience of dinner out, a movie, a walk in the park, a visit to an art gallery, or any other activity changes perspective from inward to outward. It is a break from the confines of depression.

But socialization does not have to involve going somewhere or doing something unless the person is ready for that type of interaction. A phone call or online chat with a friend is a terrify mood booster. Slipping away for a coffee break with a coworker is another way to make socialization fit into a daily routine.

Taking a step toward building new friendships can also be part of the socialization component of depression management. It may not be a strategy someone may want to try early in the treatment process but can be helpful as the depression symptoms lighten or to maintain a depression-free state of mind.

Think about getting in touch with people with whom you may have lost contact. A friend who stood by you in the tough times and enjoyed better times is someone that can be added back into your life. There's a familiarity that takes away the nervousness that comes from meeting someone new.

Expanding your existing circle of friends is also a way to use socialization as a strategy for managing depression. There are many opportunities to meet new people by volunteering at organizations for which you have a passion. If you are an animal lover, the humane society could be a place to volunteer which puts you in contact with like-minded individuals. Your place of worship can also open up new acquaintances as well as adding to the availability of people to support you in a spiritual sense.

Enrolling in a class at a college or university in the community also increases the opportunities to socialize. Sign up for an art class, a dance class, or take golf or tennis lessons. Chances are there will be people there who share the same interest.

Getting out in the community and being around people is a positive approach to controlling the symptoms of depression. It may take some effort to take the first steps, to reach out a hand in friendship, to get past the nervousness of first-time introductions. Friends add value to life and give us a companion to take on a journey.

Education

When someone has not been diagnosed with depression, the symptoms can be scary. You don't understand why you feel the way you do and why you have lost the pleasure in life. This confusion comes from not knowing what is causing the symptoms you are experiencing.

But when you have been diagnosed, there are opportunities to learn more about depression. You suddenly know what to search for in looking for information about the disorder and what you can do to make life better.

When a person is armed with information and knowledge, this is a powerful tool to use in fighting the consequences that come with the disorder. Seeking information to understand what is happening when a person is depressed is a way to manage the progression and remission of depression.

Becoming knowledgeable about depression is important for the person with depression as well as caregivers. Knowing the symptoms of depression, treatment options and resources available improve shed light on a subject for which a person may not have needed to know prior to the diagnosis.

Learning about depression also exposes the person to the stories of others who have faced similar challenges. Finding similarities and differences in these personal accounts helps to highlight the understanding that depression is much more common than people think.

Taking control of your own care and treatment options is empowering. Having a solid understanding of depression also creates teachable moments. Conversations about depression can now be supported with the knowledge acquired as part of the management strategy.

Exercise

Being active, at whatever level a person is capable of being, has long been a way to not only maintain a healthy body but a way to boost energy, mood, and balance brain and body chemistry. Regular exercise has a positive influence on self-esteem as well as reducing stress.

Research has indicated that exercise strengthens the body, improves the body's ability to metabolize food, and generates a general feeling of accomplishment. It is a route to better self-care because the attention has to be focused on the individual and not what is going on around them.

Effective exercise requires an activity that forces the heart rate to rise in response. This increases blood flow to the brain and the body. Better blood flow means the body's most vital organs are getting what they need to function properly. Studies have shown there is a correlation between physical activity and a reduced risk of cognitive function.

Exercise doesn't have to resemble an athlete training for the Olympics. Instead, it is recommended that each person finds the activity and activity level that is comfortable but effective for their personal needs. Gym memberships are one option, but so is going on a walk with a friend, joining a dance class, gardening, or taking the dog for a walk. Making exercise an enjoyable experience ensures that the person will continue to do it on a regular basis.

Choosing to park farther away from the door allows a few extra steps into a person's daily count. Opting to walk up a flight of stairs is also an effective way of adding more activity into the routine.

The connection between exercise and the brain is well documented. Being physically active stimulates the growth of new nerve cells and improves the response of synapses, the connections between the brain's cells.

Diet

A newly emerging field of psychology suggests that diet has more effect on brain function and psychological disorders than previously thought. Dubbed Nutritional Psychiatry, the idea is that a proper diet is the best way to ensure that the brain stays healthy and that the body has what it needs to circumvent adverse reactions to stressful situations.

Fuel for the brain is supplied by a person's diet. Just like the fuel put into car engines, the higher the grade, the better the performance. For the human body, however, it is all about providing the healthiest combination of foods in the right quantity. The best foods are high in vitamins, minerals, and antioxidants. These high-octane foods are free from preservatives and chemicals used in processing.

Processed foods with high sugar content are detrimental to the body because it directly affects the body's control of insulin. It also promotes inflammation and can contribute to oxidation stress. Research has noted a high sugar diet's effect on the brain as well. It has been shown that this type of diet messes with brain function and can compound the symptoms of depression and mood disorders.

Eating the proper foods ensures that all physiological functions operate properly and that all the systems release the hormones and neurotransmitters needed to keep brain chemistry balanced. As an example, consider that serotonin normalizes appetite and sleep. Serotonin is produced in the gastrointestinal tract, which is also responsible for digesting food. In addition, the bacteria in the digestive system help cleanse the body of toxins.

Research has shown that these good bacteria – probiotics – are essential to the digestive system and regulate the connections between the nerve cells and the brain. When these are at a high level, anxiety, and stress decreases and overall mental health improves.

The choice of foods can also influence brain health and reduce the risk of depression or other disorders. Opting for a so-called traditional diet, like those consumed in the Mediterranean or Japanese cultures, can reduce the risk of depression by up to 35 percent, according to research. Fruits and vegetables, and unprocessed grains are plentiful in traditional diets. So too are fish and seafood. Missing from these diets are processed foods and refined sugars.

Sleep

The obvious reason to include a healthy sleep cycle as part of a program to managing depression is that it provides the rest that the body and mind needs. Sleep also removes toxins from the brain. The buildup of these toxins happens while the person is awake and moving through the course of the day. This important brain cleansing activity is important to research when looking at the connection between a lack of sleep and depression.

When someone is not sleeping well, health experts know that there is an effect on the brain and body. Sleep deficiency weakens the ability to solve problems, notice details, and mars the power to reason.

When someone is tired, they are less productive in their jobs. Their attention is compromised, putting them at risk for an accident. Lack of sleep makes a person irritable, making interactions with others terse. Lack of sleep for an extended period is a risk factor for developing depression.

Lack of sleep can also raise the risk of getting seriously ill. It raises the risk of a person being diagnosed with heart disease and infections.

Recent research has shown that the brain's cleansing action removes a protein called a beta-amyloid, which has been detected in high quantities in the brains of Alzheimer patients. This research matches findings that suggest that the levels of beta-amyloid decrease while a person is asleep.

While a person sleeps, their body is still working. Heart rate, blood pressure, and breathing rate fluctuate throughout the night as the body balances the system. Hormones produced and circulated while the person is asleep repair cells and regulate energy use and absorption.

To keep the body and brain functioning well, experts recommend between 7 – 9 hours of sleep for adults. Teenagers function better on nine hours of sleep, children should get at least 10 hours, and infants sleep for 16 hours.

Minimizing the distractions are one way to make sure a person slips easily into sleep. The light from electronic devices is especially distracting. Drinking coffee or other caffeine-rich beverages before sleep can impact a person's ability to fall asleep. Some medications have a similar effect.

Use of Self-Love and Self-Compassion

Self-love is difficult for people who are struggling with depression. In many cases, a person's self-worth and connections to others are fractured, and even the simplest task takes tremendous effort. Putting a priority on yourself is not on the list when simply getting through the day is the challenge.

Self-Love is treating yourself with care. It's taking care of your needs so you are better able to focus on maintaining your depression or anxiety disorder. It doesn't involve lots of money or effort, just seeing that personal needs are attended to.

First, eat foods that are good for your body and your brain. You might think that a candy bar and potato chips may fill that void, but a healthy breakfast, lunch, and dinner with plenty of vegetables, fruits, whole grains, and proteins are a better choice. Make sure that the calories you provide your body are the kind that will be converted to energy and supply the vitamins and minerals your brain and body need.

Proper nutrition does not have to be complicated, especially when depression makes you not want to do much of anything. Make an effort to choose healthier quick and easy meal options/

Second, take care of your hygiene. Taking a shower, washing our hair and doing other tasks related to cleanliness is difficult for those with depression. Even a quick washing up, the use of a dry shampoo and brushing your teeth is a start. Try to do more than the bare minimum in the hygiene department, such as taking a shower or bath. A bath is particularly soothing and healing.

Soak up the Vitamin D. Get outside. Go for a walk. Sit in a park. Watch the ducks at the lake. These simple and low energy activities are great for enhancing mood. There are calmness and peaceful feelings that come from being outside. Carving out a little time during the day or evening to venture outside is good for you and shows you care about your mind, body, and spirit.

Rediscover your pleasure. Do you remember what made you happy? Was it art or poetry? Knitting or woodworking? Tinkering with your motorcycle or reading a book? Maybe it is watching made-for-television movies or relaxing to your favorite musical artist. Taking time to do things that you like to do is a great way to show yourself some love.

In a state of depression, indulging in this kind of activities may seem impossible. Simply try. Don't pressure yourself into finishing that masterpiece or the Great American Novel. Start small and enjoy the moment.

The second part of this depression management equation is self-compassion. This term means to find the dignity and wisdom in your experience and respond with kindness. Put aside the common depression-related thought that there is something wrong with you; that the world is too dark of a place; or that you have no purpose in this life. None of this is true and finding a way to show yourself some compassion will help lessen the impact of these feelings.

Touch is one way to be compassionate. One suggestion is to place your hand on your heart and take a deep breath. Or, simply brush your hand against your face or your arm. Touch stimulates the receptors in the skin, triggering a feeling of compassion.

Delve into your experiences. Writing down observations in a journal or expressing your feelings in a sketchbook. Making a connection with your own depression or negative thoughts is the same as talking with a friend and getting or giving advice.

Taking action to find solutions to your depression is also therapeutic and shows compassion. It demonstrates that you are making an effort to get better and that you are taking the steps to reclaim your power.

Practice Mindfulness – Be in the Moment

Mindfulness meditation is a way to focus on the present and not the past, in which the incidents, people or situations occurred that affected your brain and body's ability to move beyond stress and anxiety. Being in the present means taking stock of what is going on within and around your body and brain. When being mindful, the awareness of where we are, what we are doing is highlighted.

Over time, human beings who are depressed or diagnosed with an anxiety disorder have become accustomed to zeroing in on the negative aspects of life experiences. People remember when they were embarrassed, made a mistake, humiliated in front of others, or faced some other situation which allowed a criticism of themselves to be lodged in their memory. These emotionally devastating moments have become the way in which a person views themselves but are just some of the life experiences that contribute to who a person is.

Mindfulness helps by shifting focus from bad experiences to positive ones. It takes away the process of judging feelings and emotions and substitutes a more analytical and observational quality to a person's perceptions of themselves.

By eliminating the need to reflect on the past or worry about the future, mindfulness helps dissipate negative thoughts by assigning neither a positive or negative label on these. It is simply living in the present, experiencing what it is like to live in the now.

Personal perceptions of time are not simply objective observations but carry emotions as well. These memories of the past and worries about the future are linked to fears and anxiety. That makes it problematic to give these perceptions their deserved importance. Through mindfulness, enjoyment comes from the present.

Being mindful is focusing on what is happening with our bodies, our minds, and our emotions. The techniques of mindfulness are simple and do not require anyone to adopt a new belief system. It works within the structure of what a person already believes and knows about themselves.

Mindfulness forces the body to relax through focused concentration. It asks the person to be aware of their breathing, how their body curves and bends, how their heartbeat feels and sounds.

The benefit of mindfulness in the scope of managing depression is that the practice of it can naturally encourage the body to relax. When the body relaxes, the natural rhythms of the body calm the nerves and slows any signs of agitation. Less stress means the body and brain function better and the person's health, in general, improves.

Knowing how to do this gives a person with depression a tool to use when needed. Because mindfulness requires no fancy equipment or a specific place to go, it can easily be used to calm nerves or get passed a tough time of the day.

The ritual begins with deep, slow and rhythmic breaths. The eyes close and the practitioner moves through the parts of the body calling for a focus followed by relaxation. As the practitioner continues, the goal is to achieve a relaxed state from head to toe.

Mindfulness exercises are not complex and do not require an enormous amount of effort. Simple exercises can be used to achieve mindfulness meditation easily.

One technique is simply to observe the events and happening going on around you. The world moves at a very fast pace. While practicing mindfulness that pace slows down. Paying attention to how the body's five senses are responding while eating, visiting a park, or petting a dog is a mindfulness exercise that can be practiced anytime and anyplace.

A second method is to make an effort to focus on everything the practitioner does. In other words, live right now. Pamper yourself, celebrate the unpretentious joys in life, practice self-acceptance. Counter negative thoughts by focusing on deep, slow breathing to let the negative thoughts fade away.

Another exercise that mixes physical activity with mindfulness is walking meditation. According to instructions, the person should seek out a quiet place that allows about 10 – 20 feet of walking space. The person then begins to walk slowly across space. The mindfulness experience focuses on the act of walking, taking in the movements the body makes and how a person balances as the activity is underway. At the end of the path, turn around and continue to walk, constantly practicing being mindful of the experience as well as how the body responds.

Mindfulness exercises fit neatly into the sometimes-hectic schedules of everyday life. Although these meditations can be done anywhere, there is an added benefit if the mindfulness meditation is conducted outside. The suggested duration for this depression management technique is at least six months.

For more structured mindfulness exercises, such as body scan meditation or sitting meditation, you'll need to set aside time when you can be in a quiet place without distractions or interruptions. You might choose to practice this type of exercise early in the morning before you begin your daily routine.

Aim to practice mindfulness every day for about six months. Over time, you might find that mindfulness becomes effortless. Think of it as a commitment to reconnecting with and nurturing yourself.

Chapter 6: Wrapping It Up – Strategies and Resources

Depression, anxiety disorders, and phobias are not like medical illnesses—many of which there are no cures. Instead, someone who is suffering from depression or has social anxiety can take an active role in making themselves feel better.

A healthy diet, exercise, meditation, and other techniques can enhance any clinical treatments or medical interventions. While it is not wise to go through it alone without the help of a mental health professional, managing depression is a proactive and self-compassionate act.

Check Your Progression on Overcoming Social Anxiety or Depression

As with any goal a person sets for themselves, if an individual is taking steps to help themselves manage depression, it is important to know how to measure progress. Keep in mind that there will be ups and downs on the journey, but the most important consideration is to keep trying.

The easiest way to track progress is to set up a journal or record to assess what is going on. There are online resources that provide direct questions that can help track improvements and provide an objective measurement instead of a subjective one. Finding out what progress has been made is as simple as asking questions and recording the responses.

When you are training your body in preparation for an athletic event, there are measurements that can be taken to assess conditioning, tone, weight gain or loss, and heart rate among other tools to objectively measure the progress that has been made. There are no measurements that can be taken to determine if the methods being used to manage depression and anxiety are working. A person cannot simply look in the mirror and see a difference in their brain. It is important that a person listens to their thoughts to determine if their inner dialogue has changed.

Be prepared to ask yourself some tough questions and commit to answering as honestly as you can. Don't simply accept the automatic answer your mind suggests—review it and decide if it is an accurate reflection of your efforts.

Is your day-to-day functioning showing improvement? To determine if there are signs of improvement, set short-term goals, such as committing to missing fewer days of work or school or getting more sleep. As you achieve these initial short-term goals, set new ones.

Do you see an improvement with your symptoms? The Wakefield Questionnaire is a tool to rate your answers to specific questions to calculate a numeric score. This score can be compared along the way to any changes.

When completing the Wakefield Questionnaire, participants are asked to indicate on a scale of zero to three their response to the statement. One of the first questions on this form is to respond to the question I feel miserable and sad. The response includes: No, not at all (0), No, not much (1), Yes, sometimes (2), and Yes, definitely (3). Other questions include whether the person finds it easy to do the things he or she used to do, if they feel panicked or frightened for no reason, and if he or she has weeping spells or feels like crying. A similar questionnaire may have been given to the person when first consulting a medical or mental health professional.

By adding up the number value for each response, the total can determine the severity of the depression. A score above 15, indicates a person is likely depressed. Tests like the Wakefield Questionnaire are not intended to be used to diagnose clinical depression. It is a tool or gauges the possibility that a person may be depressed.

By repeating the Wakefield Questionnaire as a person continues treatment is a way to see if there has been an improvement. Although the responses are subjective to the individual, it can be useful to identify changes in responses.

Another self-test for depression takes a little different approach to the questions. The Zung Self-Rating Depression Scale asks the person to rate 20 statements on their physical and emotional state based on a scale of A little of the time, Some of the time, A good part of the time and Most of the time. Each response has a point value. Respondents are asked to answer statements such as I feel downhearted and blue; I feel I am useful and needed, and My mind is as clear as it used to be.

Examples of these and other assessments are available from multiple online sources. If using one of these tests to determine progress, make sure the same one is used each time. Different tests have different scoring systems, and that could affect the interpretation of progress in the treatment program.

Have there been any relapses? If your depression symptoms are under control, that indicates improvement. Managing depression is important because the chances of someone with depression having another occurrence of depression is increased.

Have lifestyle changes been made successfully? Changing the habits of daily life can help improve depression, especially if the situations or events that are considered stressors are under control. These lifestyle changes include being healthy and active, relating to others in a more inclusive and positive way, and dealing with stress in a proactive manner.

Lastly, consider whether your medications are causing side effects or are effective in your treatment. Treatments such as prescription drugs are designed to address some of the physiological symptoms of depression, such as stabilizing brain chemistry. If the medication side effects are complicating your life or impacting your abilities to manage your depression, your medical or mental health provider needs to know. Frustration with difficult side effects can lead to discouragement and short-circuit your progress.

There are also applications that can be downloaded on devices that are engineered to help with depression. These apps serve multiple purposes, from providing information on depression to providing tools for self-assessment. Other apps monitor physiological processes, such as heart rate, the rate of breathing and pulse. Others also have a way to determine the stress level.

To make the best choice in an app, find one that works for you that is science-based if that is what you need. Look for information on how the app obtains its information, such as from a consultation with medical or mental health experts.

There are a variety of apps that focus on the various treatment options, such as one that addresses cognitive behavior therapy. An app dealing with this treatment option provides information on the therapy and has a test to help a person determine the severity of the depression. This is an electronic version of the paper versions of the various depression questionnaires. As a tool to measure progress, the app has a tracking component to record positive thoughts and overall mood. It also includes guided meditations for those with depression.

One app that has received an endorsement from mental health professionals who were also designers of the program is called MoodKit. This app is designed to help someone overcome a bad mood by providing mood improvement activities. There are other apps that provide similar support. The journal tool and built-in thought tracker on MoodKit and other apps provide a resource for recording thoughts or observations. Its primary function is to elevate the mood of the user.

Other apps, such as Daylio, allows the user to record their mood, using an emoji-like system. Tools built into apps like this provide a visual record of the emotional swings. Like many of these self-assessment apps, there is usually a journaling feature.

Remember that an app is not a replacement for professional mental health advice. Consult with your doctor before following any suggestions made by an online or mobile source.

Talk to Someone

Anyone who is experiencing any of the symptoms of depression or an anxiety disorder should remember that they do not have to go it alone. In fact, being able to talk about the diagnosis or the challenges is both therapeutic and essential in getting the help a person needs in managing depression.

Reaching out to family and friends is a convenient way to begin the conversation about your mental health. These are often the people you trust the most, the ones whom you know have your back when things get tough. Consider the family members who have the personality to be the most supportive. Someone who is judgmental or pessimistic may not be the person to whom you open up to.

Finding the words to express how depression or anxiety is impacting your life is not an easy task. There is no set of instructions to follow to convey what you feel, what you experience or what obstacles you scale every day. Remember that everyone is an expert on themselves and depression is different for everyone.

If family and friends are an uncomfortable option to begin a conversation about your mental health challenges, seek out another person you trust. A teacher is one option; a member of the clergy can be another. Perhaps there is a counselor or medical professional you have a rapport with that could be someone to listen as you vocalize what you are feeling inside.

Bringing another person or persons into the loop is a good first step toward finding a way out. Giving your inner thoughts a voice can be therapeutic.

Don't be afraid to ask for help and support. Developing a strong support network and making use of their love and commitment to your health is vital and an important treatment tool.

Aside from family and friends, one important person to include in these conversations about depression is the primary care doctor. The symptoms of depression are similar to symptoms for other health concerns. A primary care doctor can narrow down the diagnoses to make sure the problems the patient is experiencing is related to depression.

When you need to find a new doctor for any reason, take some time to find a practitioner that can relate to you and with whom you are comfortable. You will be sharing some very personal information, and the ability to trust the medical professional is important.

A medical doctor may be only the first step in finding your way to treatment and relief from depression. You may be referred to a mental health professional for further evaluation. Be prepared to talk about family history of depression or other mental illness, as well as the list of your symptoms.

Finding a support group is a good option in finding people to talk to about depression. The experience of sharing information, feelings, strategies, and tips about treatments and managing depression from those who are living with it like you are is encouraging and helpful.

Talk to your support group about the challenges you face and the treatment plan that has been put in place by your mental health team. Talk about what triggers anxiety or stress and seek their support in helping you make better lifestyle choices.

While some support groups meet in person, there are other options for someone who would be more comfortable participating in an online chat room for people with depression. It is important to look for a chat room moderated or affiliated with a mental health organization. The online chat room also provides more anonymity in conversations while providing a community of people who can identify with a person's struggles with depression.

Chat rooms that are moderated are a safe place to share experiences. Open social media platforms are not. It is important to remember that very few of the chat rooms will have a mental health professional as the moderator. While most do their best to maintain a safe, polite environment, there is no guarantee that discussions may not turn hostile. Chat rooms should be used as an additional resource in addition to seeking help from professionals in the mental health or medical community.

Talk therapy is one of the treatment options available in the fight against depression. Also known as psychotherapy, it involves a client and a therapist. The therapy session usually lasts no more than an hour and can take different directions, depending on the treatment plan or any current crises in a person's life that require attention.

There are several types of psychotherapy. Variations include cognitive-behavioral, interpersonal and problem-solving therapies.

Access to a therapist in a digital world is a possibility. Research indicates that many people achieve positive results with online therapy programs, but mental health practitioners caution people from going this route without checking credentials and clearing the treatment program with your doctor.

When someone is talking to you about their depression, there is no script to follow. The best way to respond is to listen to what they say and show them you support them. Assuring them that you are ready to help in any way you can or reminding them that they do not have to handle this alone are positive ways to respond.

It's also acceptable to ask someone if they are OK, even if the inquiry seems awkward or is uncomfortable. It opens a door that a person suffering from depression needs to walk through. Avoid saying that you know how they feel. Don't discount what they are experiencing by saying, "everyone gets depressed" or "think happy thoughts." And don't tell them they have nothing to be depressed about.

What happens when a person's mental health has reached a crisis stage, such as the contemplation of suicide? At this life-or-death moment, it is even more important for the person contemplating taking this step to reach and talk about their feelings. If that person is reluctant to tell family, friends or their support group, there are still people who can help.

The National Suicide Prevention Crisis Center maintains a toll-free hotline to provide that extra help at what could be the darkest moment of someone's depression. These crisis centers are located in communities and are often part of the county or local behavioral health systems. Most of these centers are structured as non-profit organizations, with both mental health professionals and volunteers available 24-hours a day, seven days a week. These centers do not close for holidays and the services provided are free to those who need it.

When making a call to the hotline, the person in crisis will be directed to someone who can help them almost immediately. There is no travel to a medical center, or the need to make multiple calls to find someone to talk to. The person who answers the call is trained in how to offer help. The person who answers the call listens to the caller, determines the effects the problem is having on the individual and provides support. The caller may also be given resources to help in this situation.

Talking about depression or social anxiety is not easy to do. There are still prejudices against people with mental illnesses, and the subject makes people uncomfortable. Sometimes, however, a little discomfort goes a long way towards healing. People who are struggling with depression feel alone, isolated and as if it was a case of themselves against the world. Talking about depression and how it affects a person brings other people into the struggle. There is safety in numbers, and there is healing too.

Get Your Family and Friends On Board!

When navigating the choppy waters of depression, don't be afraid to build a support group around you of your family and friends. Having people that you trust and those who care about you provides strength and courage to face the challenges each day with depression holds.

A strong support system is an essential part of the recovery process. A support group is a vital part of managing depression, according to research. The positive benefits include improved ways of coping with stressful situations and challenges and provide encouragement to make healthier choices. Support groups also help reduce anxiety and depression.

The size and makeup of the group is a personal decision. Small or large, those who are a part of the support group should be committed to helping their loved one find balance and a way to lift depression. Some people in the group may provide emotional support and others may be better at providing financial support or help in other ways.

Avoid people who may make a situation more stressful. Rule out those who are negative. The best support group members are those with a healthy outlook on life and those who are positive in their thoughts and interactions.

The people who come together in support of a loved one who is diagnosed with depression don't necessarily have to be close friends or family. Neighbors and clergy members are also viable options. Pets can be part of the support a person receives.

When a loved one is diagnosed with depression, it affects those they love. Family and friends can lend their support by making sure their loved one gets medical attention and a diagnosis. A person with depression may need a loved one to come with them to a doctor's appointment. They may also need to be reminded to stick with the treatment plan or may need help finding alternative options.

If you are helping to a family member or friend with their depression, keep your conversations judgment-free and be patient as they work through setbacks and challenges. Be emotionally supportive of their efforts and offer encouragement.

Remember that this is a struggle for your family member or friend, but it will also be difficult for you. A person with depression may need support for an extended period. As a caregiver, take time for yourself and don't neglect your own care.

Here are some other suggestions to make the interaction more positive and effective:

- When talking with your loved one, listen carefully to what they say
- Don't ignore any comment about suicide
- Report any suicide warning signs to their doctor
- Offer hope but don't dismiss how they are feeling
- Be there to help them get to doctor's appointments or other therapy
- Involve your family member in activities, such as going for a walk.
- Reiterate that depression will lift over time with treatment

There are some other ways in which family and friends can demonstrate their support and commitment to their loved one's recovery.

Conduct some research on depression. Understanding the basics of the disorder your loved one is going through is a great way to support them. Once you gain an understanding, it is easier to know how you can help and how to verbally express your commitment to their journey towards healing.

Consider becoming a Mental Health First Aid responder, or at least sign up to take the class. Administered by the National Council for Behavioral Health, this class provides participants with the knowledge to identify risk factors, note warning signs and take action when these signs manifest. In addition, participants learn about treatment options, how to determine if someone is having a mental health crisis, choose interventions to help, and how to connect with resources for the individual.

A Mental Health First Aid responder recognizes the importance of early detection and quick intervention. It helps them identify the patterns and symptoms of several mental health disorders, including anxiety disorders and depression. This information equips the family or friend with fact-based information to better serve as a resource their loved one can count on.

Once you've made the commitment to be there for your family member or friend, make sure you reach out to them regularly. Check on how they are, issue an invitation to hang out or offer to help with errands and daily responsibilities.

Depression and anxiety may be different for everyone, but that doesn't mean the fight with these disorders has to be a solitary one. Bringing family and friends to stand with you makes the journey toward a solution a better one. A helping hand to get you through the day, a hand on the shoulder for support, and a sympathetic ear to get you through an emotional crisis are invaluable.

Talking about depression and anxiety is essential in bringing these inner thoughts to light. Once the negative thoughts are out in the light, it is easier to see the fallacies these thoughts hold. Talk is cheap unless it is to share your struggles and impart knowledge to others. Then talk is priceless.

Organizations and Resources

One of the advantages of the digital world is that information and education is literally at our fingertips. As with anything found on the internet, it is important to check the source's information and determine if the site is credible.

Another cautionary warning is to make sure any suggested therapies for depression or anxiety are approved by your own mental health or medical provider.

The following are some of the national organizations that can educate and provide links to resources for depression and anxiety.

- National Alliance on Mental Illness 1-800-950-NAMI (1-800-950-6264)
- Anxiety and Depression Association of America 1-240-485-1001
- National Institute of Mental Health 1-866-615-6464

- Centers for Disease Control and Prevention Division of Mental Health 1-800-CDC-INFO (1-800-232-4636)
- American Psychological Association 1-800-374-2721
- American Psychiatric Association 1-703-907-7300
- American Foundation for Suicide Prevention 1-800-273-TALK (1-800-273-8255)
- Depression and Bipolar Support Alliance 1-800-826-3632
- Erika's Lighthouse 847-386-6481. This site builds awareness around teenage depression.
- Families for Depression Awareness 1-781-890-0220

Conclusion

Thank you for making it through to the end of Social Anxiety: Guide to Overcome Anxiety and Shyness.
Let's hope it was informative and able to provide you with all of the tools you need to achieve your goals—whatever they may be.

There is a lot of information packed into these six chapters. That's only because there is a lot of information about depression and social anxiety. As one of the most common mental health concerns, depression has very serious consequences for those who struggle with the disorder. Suicide is a grim consequence. Prolonged depression can also lead to medical-related illnesses and disease, such as diabetes and heart disease among others.

For the person who is challenged every day with depression, or the person who suffers severe anxiety when forced to interact with others, this book provides hope and encouragement in the knowledge that they are not alone. The information in this book illustrates that there are many ways to take control and manage their depression. It points out that there are options in therapy, in lifestyle choices, and in finding a way past the anxiety and emotional darkness.

For the family or friend of a person who is diagnosed with depression, this book offers insight and perspectives into these mental health diagnoses. With this knowledge comes the possibility that family and friends can provide the support and understanding to see their loved one through this tough struggle.

Thank you

CPSIA information can be obtained
at www.ICGtesting.com
Printed in the USA
BVHW041115100720
583432BV00010B/106